THE C  Y

Shaping the Culture of Community

By Scot Conway, Ph.D., J.D.

Be Ohana
Build Ohana
Bring Ohana
to the World!

Aloha!
Scot Conway

THE OHANA WAY BOOK
Shaping the Culture of Community

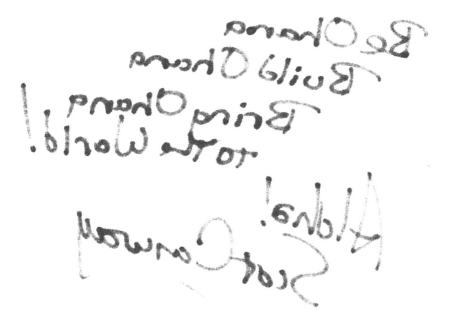

Please be kind and review this book
Let us know something you learned you thought was great!

Find all of Dr. Scot Conway's books on Amazon
Author Page: http://amzn.com/e/B009VNPT44
Or search "Scot Conway"

NEXT LEVEL LEADERSHIP
www.4P360.com

Dr. Scot Conway's trademark Leadership System.
Powerful, Practical, Principled, Positive Leadership of Self
and Others in 360 Degrees. See website for details.

More training programs by Scot Conway.
www.ScotWith1T.com
www.ScotConway.org
www.ScotConway.com

A growing collection of video lessons may be found on
YouTube: https://www.youtube.com/user/ScotAConway

For martial arts:
www.GQDojo.com

For ministry:
www.QXChurch.org

For Not-for-Profit Projects:
www.QuestXTeam.org

Table of Contents

5

PART SEVEN: MAKING IT HAPPEN 175

CHAPTER ZERO

HOW TO READ THIS BOOK

This book is meant to be easy reading.

It's short enough to be read in one or two sittings. The writing is intended to be straightforward and easy to understand. It's organized simply so you can come back to it any time and find the part you're looking for.

Some of the ideas may seem obvious. Others will be profound and might even be a little mind-bending. Those ideas might be a little more challenging to wrap your head around. It's worth it! What may be obvious to you might be mind-bending to someone else, and the same is true is reverse.

In our experience, everyone already does some of what you'll find in this book. Also based upon our experience, many aspects are brand new to a lot of people.

GETTING THE MOST OUT OF THE BOOK

First, just flip through the book.

Take a look at the Table of Contents, look at the chapter headings, and glance at section headings and other parts that stand out to you.

Just spend a few minutes with the book and set it aside. If you want to get to it right away, just leave it aside for five or ten minutes. Otherwise, it's best to glance at it either at night just before bed or in the morning just after waking. Then get to it later in the day or sometime the next day.

What you're doing is letting your brain form a "mental bookshelf" for the material. Your brain has seen what's in the book so it knows what to expect. It sets up empty mental-files ready to be filled with the information it knows to expect.

Second, read it through.

You can read it all in one sitting if you like. It's organized to start simply and then dive deeper. The opening sections introduce ohana as a concept and then give a very surface-insight into it.

Then the sections for each element of OHANA follow. You can read just one of "the five" and ponder it for that day. Or you could read all five of them. That's up to you.

Our suggestion is that when you get to an idea that is a bit of a stretch for you, stop there for a while. Give yourself time to think about it.

Grasping the ideas intellectually should be easy enough. We try to be clear in our discussion of ideas. It's the application that is very individual. It's unique to you, your life, and your personal history. You might realize how similar or how different your personal experience has been. You might ponder to what extent, if any, you might choose to move closer to the ideal discussed.

When you get to a section that's particularly thought provoking, stop at that chapter and let it sink in that day.

When you've paused because a chapter prompted some deeper thinking, when you resume reading, re-read that chapter. Then continue.

Third, skim the book again.

After you're done reading, go back through the book again. This should only take a few minutes. Just flip through the pages and mentally note if the ideas there are familiar to you. Use bookmarks to hold the places you might want to go back to and read again. Re-read any section about which you might want to think about more deeply.

That's the process of reading the book. It's actually almost exactly the same technique we teach to high school and college students for studying their textbooks. This system lets you increase your retention with very little adjustment in your strategy! Feel free to use it with any reading material.

UNDERSTAND WHAT WE MEAN

The way we use language to describe things may be a little different than how you might use the same words. It's certainly more specific than many people experience. We try to define our terms as we go.

For example, some people use "aggressive" in a way we do not. For us, "aggressive" is "moving without respect for others." We define what we mean. Someone might say, "that's not what aggressive is!"

We define "assertive" as "moving forward on purpose with respect for others." Aggressive might be forward movement, but it could also be backwards (as in damaging to relationship). It has its own agenda, and respect for others is largely incidental. Assertiveness presumes there's a forward (a goal), and that other people are innately important and should be respected. That's how we use these words.

It's totally okay if you don't use our vocabulary the exact same way we do. Just learn the idea. Call it whatever you want in your own life. Just know that we use words to mean certain things. When we use those words, we mean those certain things.

Just let us mean what we mean. In time, the little bit of extra precision of our vocabulary with pretty clean definitions lets us all be on the same page. That way we're not getting lost arguing over words when what we're really after is ideas!

Often, people get bogged down debating things when the outcome of those debates changes nothing. Focus on understanding what we mean. In fact, that's a good general policy. Any time before you consider getting into a debate about a word or a label or a generalization or exceptions, ask yourself "Is it important right here, right now, for us to understand this point?" If it is, go ahead. If not, please stop. Feel free to use that question with others, too.

A thing we've periodically observed is that some of us are trained to use petty arguments to avoid bigger issues. In this case, if you catch yourself quibbling about the use of a word or how we express an idea, pause and take a look to see if you have a challenge with the idea itself. There's a chance you're just doing what you were trained to do so you can avoid thinking too hard. A lot of us got taught to do that. When we realize we're doing it, we can decide to skip the petty and take a wiser look at the important lesson.

IT IS ABOUT ME; IT IS NOT ABOUT "THEM"

When we read about new ideas, it's very natural to read and think, "Yeah, so-and-so needs to know this!" Or we might think, "I wish my parents did this for me when I was a kid!"

Basically, it's easy to see what other people should do differently. It's easy to see what other people should have known or should have done better. Other people are who they are. They do what they do. By reading a book or attending a seminar, my new learning doesn't change who they are or what they did.

It CAN change me, though! So that's my focus.

I look for what I can learn. I look for what I can do better. I look for where I can be a better example.

I grow first. I make sure I understand first. If I can share some helpful ideas in a way that illuminates, that can be helpful. It's part of "Be a light, not a judge" and "be a safe person."

We make sure our relationship makes us well-worth listening to. Note, we say "relationship," not "our knowledge makes us worth listening to." There's an old saying, "people don't care how much you know until they know how much you care."

Depending upon our relationship, the best we might do is be a better example. Then we can explain the example we're being.

My job is to BE Ohana.

If there are ten of us, each of us waiting for everyone else to go first, no one is going. If there are ten of us, each of us practicing Ohana, then every one of us has nine people doing for us! So we just go first. We ALL go first.

We walk the path. We SHOW others the way. We don't just TELL them; we SHOW them. That's the basic definition of "sensei," that senior person who teaches because they did it first.

ENJOY THE ADVENTURE

OHANA can be absolutely transformational. Parts of Ohana might be the exact opposite of how you grew up. Bits might be very, very different from what your life looks like right now. If this is true, there is a good chance you have years of training and practice doing things a way you now want to change.

You'll also find that parts are exactly how you do it – or very close. Those parts will give you a vocabulary to discuss it with others.

We can build Ohana. We build family. We become more than fellow members in a dojo. We go past teammates, co-workers, and friends. We even go past what passes for family these days. We talk about families being dysfunctional so much that dysfunctional is considered normal now!

Whether you're exactly on course or you find a few areas to tweak, enjoy the adventure. Where radical change might be required, there are tools for that, too. I've authored books and produced programs on a great many topics, proving an abundance of tools for your personal growth.

Whether you're making tiny adjustments or huge changes, enjoy the process. It's an adventure! All of us have experiences and insights as we go through life. That changes us. Since we're going to change anyway, we may as well change on purpose! Then we can pick a direction that we really like! Ohana is one of those great directions.

Enjoy the adventure to the OHANA Ideal!

PART ONE
OHANA BASICS

CHAPTER ONE

OHANA

BACKGROUND

My mother grew up in Hawaii. My parents met in the Aloha State and that's also where I was born.

I was a kid in a huggie-kissie home. I got tons of hugs and kisses as I grew up. I was told I was loved and shown that I was loved. I had no doubts of this truth as I grew up.

Of course, like any kid, I messed up sometimes. My mother's favorite line when I'd do some stupid was "Why would a smart kid like you do such a stupid thing?" She attached "smart" to my identity. I was smart. Only "the thing" was stupid. The "right answer" was "I didn't think about it first" (I was learning to think about things before I did them).

"So what does a smart kid do when he realizes he's doing a stupid thing?" The right answer here was "He stops, fixes it, and does better next time."

That pretty much encapsulates the theme of how my mother raised me. My brother and I were smart kids. We were "better than that" when we did dumb things. We "knew better" when we did something that she knew she or our dad had already taught us.

Then there was training. We were actively taught skills. I stood by my father as he grilled food and showed me how to cook on a grill. I watched my mother cook up "oh whatever" from seemingly random ingredients found in the kitchen. I learned to do yard work, housework, laundry, cooking, cleaning – all the skills needed to run a household.

I was the quiet kid through elementary school. By high school, though, all that had changed. I was one of the key leaders in a large group of friends that met at the location in our high school called "Henry's Hut." That became our symbol. We became known as "The Hut."

What set The Hut apart from other cliques around campus was that we had no theme. What we used to say was "the only thing we have in common is that none of us has anything in common with all of us."

The Hut had a variety of races, a variety of religions, and a variety of political and philosophical views. Some of our members had GPAs over 4.0, and at least one of our members wasn't going to graduate until he transferred to a special school that could help him. Some of us were para-military and went on to serve, and some were pacifists. Some did the whole party-scene, and some wouldn't have known what drugs were what even if you tried to explain them.

One of our members was very pro-Hitler because she had learned about Hitler when she grew up in Iran and only learned about what he did for the German economy and how he rallied the country. In her school as a child, the Holocaust was a footnote. Of course, we had a more conventional American view. For us, the Holocaust was Hitler's legacy and him saving the German economy was the footnote. With so many Jews in our group, that lead to some lively discussions! Yet, there was no name-calling, no judging, and no accusations.

These were a few of the basic rules:

Show the respect and acceptance you expect to receive.
Never force anyone to do anything they disagree with.
Connect where you connect and leave the rest out.

At the time, we had no idea how revolutionary it was. Our group of 70-or-so teens to follow rules like this seemed self-evidently right to us. On Wednesday, I could declare a "Hut Party" at school and have 70 people at my house on Friday. They all knew the Conway House Rules: No under-aged drinking at my house, no drugs (or I call the police and testify against you), and smoking was allowed on the sidewalk (the law let minors smoke in those days). We'd still have a good-sized party with a lot of people having a good time!

19

Our basic rules worked for us. They were enormously powerful.

Unfortunately, when the bulk of us graduated in the classes of 1983 and 1984, we scattered to the winds. Some of us went to the military, some to universities ranging from local community colleges to MIT, Berkeley, and Stanford, and many of us got jobs and started adult living.

Some of us saw one another for years afterwards, but, in time, it all faded away. There was one place the ideals learned in the House of Conway and The Hut continued: The Guardian Quest Dojo.

It combined some of the ideals of Hawaiian Culture, my childhood home, and my high school circle of friends. Like a martial art, we've codified it so anyone can learn what we mean. That's what this book is about: Building a culture of family... of OHANA (caps intentional).

OHANA INTRODUCTION

"Ohana means family. Family means no one gets left behind or forgotten." – Lilo and Stitch

Thanks to the movie Lilo and Stitch, popular culture has a basic definition of ohana. The movie came out in 2002, and children born many years after still know the definition of ohana from the movie. Such is the power of Disney. I sat down with five and six year olds, and when I ask them if they know what ohana means, they do. They have the Disney definition down perfect!

The definition really is pretty good. In the movie, ohana includes Lilo and her sister Nani. Stitch is adopted as ohana, which drives much of the story. Over the course of the series, ohana includes David, Jumba, Pleakley, and all the other 625 experiments. It illustrates that ohana goes way beyond those you're related to by blood or marriage. It's those you're "related to" because of love.

"Calabash cousin" is part of ohana. This Hawaiian custom (and by no means unique to Hawaii) is that close friends become cousins. Older men and women are often auntie or uncle. "Family" is a bond of blood and marriage, of course, and good friends also become family.

While you definitely find this extended, deeper meaning of family in Hawaii, you find it in many other places. In contemporary mainland culture, the *Fast and Furious* series of movies uses a similar concept. Dominic Toretto (Vin Diesel) says to Deckard Shaw (Jason Statham), "I don't have friends; I got family." (*Furious 7*, 2015). "Family" is more than blood for a lot of people.

Many of us grew up considering some of our best friends brothers and sisters. Some of us grew up calling our friends' mothers "mom." We all understand that people consider friends we consider more than friends. They can become family. We use phrases like "brother from another mother" and "sister from another mister."

With Ohana, "real" relationships trump "legal" relationships. You can search back through blood and marriage and find the common ancestor and you're legally related. With Ohana, you can be cousins without any regard to whether you actually related. Some cousins may or may not be related. They don't know. They don't care. They're cousins no matter what.

At the Guardian Quest Dojo, anyone can show up and take lessons.

Becoming part of the family is optional.

Some do. Some don't.

We almost stumbled into Ohana, our most unexpected treasure. We built Ohana because, simply, I wanted it.

I wanted to be the person I wished I had in my life when I was young. I wanted to teach my students the things I wished I had learned. I actually did learn a lot of it when I was young. Most of it came later.

GRANDMOTHER EYES

My mother became a grandmother. With "grandmother's eyes" she saw things she had not seen as a mother. She saw that some things were critically important that she hadn't given much attention. She saw that other things weren't nearly as big a deal as she thought. We were close enough that I got the benefit of her new insights and realizations.

So I showed up with "grandfather eyes" to teach. It was a joke that I would hold a grapefruit in the hand pondering the impact on generations to come if I ate or it didn't eat it. Okay... maybe the joke was funny because it was so true!

There we were weaving together three ideals: The House of Conway, The Hut, and "Grandmother's Eyes." What did it all make? Ohana!

As a master of martial arts, I started off with an assumption that everyone who came wanted to learn the physical art of protecting oneself and others. When my students had to use their skill and successfully stopped criminal after criminal, I thought, "I am doing my job." We had a great art with powerful techniques. We taught well and our students learned.

In the first 25 years of me teaching, we tallied 30 criminal assaults against my students, with 30 successful defenses. Yes, a lot of that is skill. I readily admit that a lot of it is luck, too. When a particular white belt learned a defense against a punch, and two weeks later the criminal that attacks punches at him, that's luck.

As it turns out, that's only one small part of my job. Only about one-in-three people ever gets targeted with violence at a level where they need that kind of self-protection skill. Those that face violence more often are usually in a dangerous environment: a particularly bad neighborhood, a dangerous job, or an abusive relationship. The majority of people manage to get through their whole lives without ever being seriously attacked (serious defined as requiring medical attention afterwards).

Another part of my job is transformation. I knew that. I teach a "lifestyle martial art," meaning it's more about teaching people how to live than it is how to fight.

A long, long time ago I learned this concept: "A good teacher will show you how to fight; a great teacher will show you how to live." There's an incredible amount of transformational material in what I do. By way of example, some of it is so powerful that it can even teach your body to stop having allergic reactions. I know, crazy stuff!

Here's the big surprise. Over my first quarter century of teaching, the single most common thing that gets said is this: "I love my dojo family."

It's about family. It's about Ohana.

I had no idea how important this would be when I started. In fact, as important as transformation and effective martial arts are, what people crave most is the community we have.

We're open to anyone. Not everyone wants to be a part of the family. That's okay. Some people would rather just train and go home.

Those who become family remain family. There are those who have left us because they got stationed elsewhere, or they moved out of State, or, in some cases, they even moved to another country!

You can tell how important our family is to us and others by the number of people who come visit when they're in town. Sometimes old students get in touch online to ask for the same kind of advice they might seek if they still lived here and trained with us. Some leave for a while and return.

Ohana means family. It means you are more important than just your role here. You are more important than just a tuition check. You matter as a whole person. You matter. And if you're the type of person who likes that and gives back to others, then you can quickly and easily be ohana, too!

This is our culture. Feel free to adopt any or all of it for your own!

CHAPTER TWO

OHANA

THE FOUNDATION

Here's the really, really short version, right out of a Disney movie:

OHANA – "Ohana means family, and family means no one gets left behind... or forgotten." (*Lilo and Stich*, 2002)

Ohana means family. Family is much more than those related by blood or marriage. It does include them, of course. It also includes friends, calabash cousins, and anyone with whom you share enough in common that you might consider them ohana.

One aspect of this shows up in a simple term: "Hawaii." When people connected to the islands do nice things for one another, they sometimes call it simply "Hawaii." When someone used to live in Hawaii but they have left behind that kind of natural generosity common in the islands, they sometimes say "They aren't Hawaii anymore."

NO ONE GETS LEFT BEHIND

Kathleen looked like someone punched her in the gut. She looked half-dazed. Her knees were weak. Something happened. Whatever it was, it was bad.

We didn't know her much more than as a dinner companion on the cruise ship. The ship sat ten to a table. On the first night, we made a game of getting to know everyone's name and who was with whom. Kathleen and her teenaged son, Jim, were two of our eight tablemates.

I asked her what was wrong as a crewmember helped her to a comfortable place to sit down. Kathleen couldn't tell us the whole story herself. She could hardly breathe. With her permission, the crewmember told us what happened.

"Her son didn't make it back to the ship. He's lost in Hilo." No wonder she was almost in shock!

Hilo is the biggest city on the "Big Island" of the State of Hawaii. The cruise ship had put into port that morning and set sail again at 5pm. The next stop was on the far side of the island at 7am the next morning. Somehow, Jim didn't make it back to the ship!

As Kathleen settled herself, she explained that Jim had asked to go shopping. He had money, he knew where the ship was, he knew what he wanted to get and where to go for it. He promised he'd be back early. Against the judgment of her fears, she decided to give her son some extra freedom.

Everything that could be done from aboard ship had been done. In Kona, she planned to disembark and go back to Hilo to find her son. The police had been notified. The cruise line had been notified. The only thing there was left to do was for Kathleen to try to make it through the night and get back to Hilo to find Jim.

The next morning the ship docked in Kona. Kathleen was on the first transfer to the shore. There was already the hustle and bustle of the cruise-ship-in-port activity at the shore. Even so, she saw him there standing on the dock waving. It took an extra moment to make sure her mom-brain wasn't seeing what she had wished for all night.

It was Jim! He had somehow beaten the ship to the other side of the island!

HOW HER SON BEAT US TO THE OTHER SIDE

He got to Kona before the ship did. He made it all the way to the opposite side of the island, fed and rested, and was waiting on the dock for his mother.

How? This was Hawaii!

We later learned that Jim mixed up the departure time in Hilo with the arrival time in Kona. He thought the ship sailed at 7, so he showed up at 6. The ship had already been gone for an hour! The driver, realizing the ship had already sailed, asked if it had been to the other side of the island, yet. He knew that ships put into both ports, so if this was the first stop on the Big Island, it would be on the other side of the island in the morning.

The taxi driver took Jim home to hang out with his own teenaged sons. He let the boy hang out with his family, have dinner with them, and sleep over. In the morning, the boy had breakfast with the family.

In the early morning, the cab driver drove the boy all the way across the island in time to meet the ship when it put into port. The fare would have been hundreds of dollars that the boy did not have, but that didn't matter.

This was Hawaii. A boy had to be reunited with his mother. A family had a cruise to finish. This was a chance for "Hawaii" to shine!

Kathleen had no words for the relief and love that exploded from her heart when she saw Jim. She thanked the cab driver profusely who would not accept any more money for his services. His joy was getting the family back together so they could continue their vacation.

That's Hawaii. That's Ohana.

Someone didn't make it to the ship and got left behind. A Hawaiian family had the ability to get the boy to the ship so he could catch up. No one gets left behind - not if we can help it!

The idea of "no one gets left behind" means you don't get "ditched." It means you don't get kicked out of the group. It means no one becomes the target or the butt of jokes. You're not bullied.

If we extend it to romance, it means no one "ghosts" (what we used to call "dumping") – meaning no one just disappears without at least having a talk about it.

YOU CAN STAY

Of course people get to decide if they want to stay behind. That's different.

"No one gets left behind" does not mean you're not allowed to stay behind. If you don't want to come along, ohana doesn't drag you along against your will.

The exception, of course, is parents with their minor children. Then you might get dragged along, like it or not. If so, you may as well step up your own game. BE ohana. Be part of your family!

For most things, though, coming along or staying behind is a choice you get to make. Ohana won't ditch you. Ohana won't drag you along kicking and screaming either. It's up to you. You're invited.

Behavior might be kicked out. Sometimes some people insist on behaving badly. Like a job at which someone does not do the job, either the behavior needs to be upgraded or the person is deciding for themselves to not be part of the team. It's the same with Ohana. If someone decides that violating the principles is more important to them than the ohana, that's up to them. Ohana will give them a chance. What they do with that chance it up to them.

NO ONE GETS FORGOTTEN

It's the nature of life that priorities ebb and flow. Life just gets busy sometimes. It's very easy for people to go weeks, months or even years without seeing one another.

Going away to college, being stationed overseas, or moving too far away to visit can interrupt any relationship for some period of time. Sometimes a change in a season of life interrupts and changes relationships. When someone gets married, has a child (or *another* child), starts a new job, or gets involved in any major projects, relationships can be interrupted.

Part of "no one is forgotten" means you can pop back up any time and expect to be just as liked and loved as you were when you left. It helps if you handled your departure well. Remember the "no one gets left behind" means you don't "ghost," you don't just vanish without explanation.

Of course it's possible that if someone handled their time toward the end of the relationship poorly, that may have done damage. Whatever someone does becomes part of the history of the relationship. That demonstration of what to expect gets factored in the relationship going forward. But you also recognize that people learn and grow. While history might be one of the best ways guess at the future, the past does not equal the future. It might give us cause to tread a bit more cautiously. We can let go of a past and give someone a chance to show they've grown.

Part of "no one is forgotten" means when you show up again, you're always welcomed back. It's the kind of friendship where you can go without seeing a friend for years, but when you visit it's like you never left.

To be honest, it's possible if you've been gone for a while, we might not remember you. That's okay. Just re-introduce yourself, and you're right back in the family. It's easy! That's the way ohana works.

CHAPTER THREE

O.H.A.N.A.

"I knew I'd feel better as soon as I got here… and I do."

Brielle worked and went to school. Her days were often long and sometimes exhausting. This particular day was bad. School was hard. She failed a test in a class required for her major.

Work was terrible. A vulgar customer hit on her and nothing polite she said was getting him to stop. Another customer yelled at her for what turned out to have been the customer's own mistake.

It was one of those days when life just piled on and kept piling on. She recently was sick on top of it. "Probably all the stress" she concluded. Physically, she just wanted to go home and go to bed. Home had stresses of its own. She wasn't in a hurry to get there.

She needed her ohana. She raced to where they were. As she walked in the door, she could almost feel the stress being peeled off her back. It fell to the ground outside to sink away.

Brielle was with people who she knew were her partners. She knew she was with this special family she had chosen.

O.H.A.N.A.

Ohana means family. Family includes those bonded by affection and something in common.

It represents an ideal that we illustrate by using ohana as an acronym. Technically, that means we should always have periods between our latters as in O.H.A.N.A., but we often dispense with the periods and just write it OHANA or even just capitalize Ohana. This way we know we're talking about our five-part acronym.

OHANA means:

O-Oasis
H-Harmony
A-Assertiveness
N-Nobility
A-Aloha

Each one of these elements has a more complete, deeper expression than this (which we explore in future chapters). As a starting place, this is what we mean:

OASIS – Be a Refreshing Refuge. Being an Oasis and helping create an Ohana Oasis means I always make it better by being here. I help create a refuge from the usual, the annoying and the difficult.

HARMONY – Embrace Infinite Diversity in Infinite Combinations Aimed at Greatness. Great music is made from melody and harmony. Many instruments, notes, and singers work together to make all sorts of different and amazing music. Harmony means we don't have to be alike to be together.

ASSERTIVENESS – Moving Forward on Purpose with Respect for Others. We Live Life on Purpose. We live assertively, learn assertively and love assertively. We practice assertive listening, assertive relatlonships, assertive parenting, and assertiveness in any and all areas of life.

NOBILITY – Be our Highest and Best Selves. The metaphor of the Royal Knight dives deep into our ideals of princeliness and princessliness in their highest and best forms. We pursue knightly chivalry and samurai bushido in service to high ideals.

ALOHA – Love in All Its Many Meanings and Manifestations. Love is I want the best for you, I want to be the best for you, and I want you to have transcendent joy. Aloha also includes hello and goodbye in Hawaiian.

OHANA FIVE BY FIVE

Each one of the five larger ideas has within it five ideas that fit the theme. We call this the "Ohana Five By Five."

The term "five by five" means things are the best quality. It comes from radio communication as a sign that the signal was perfectly readable and very strong. Our Ohana Five By Five is meant to be easily read, clearly understood, and very strong for building powerful, positive relationship when applied.

The Ohana Five by Five builds from the five ideals of Ohana: Oasis, Harmony, Assertiveness, Nobility, and Aloha. We'll dive more deeply into each ideal first, and then we'll go into each of the five by five.

The Ohana Five By Five are:

OASIS
Be a Refreshing Refuge.
    1:      Win/Win or No Deal
    2:      Give to Givers Who Give
    3:      Be a Safe Person; Create a Safe Place
    4:      Resolve (My, Your, Our), Concede (Trade Wins), Compromise
    5:      Leave No Trace; Better Than You Found It

HARMONY
Embrace Infinitely Diversity in Infinite Combinations Aimed at Greatness.
    1:      Differences are Issues to Navigate, Not Causes for Condemnation
    2:      Bad Things are Problems to Solve, Not Causes for Condemnation
    3:      More For, Less Against. Focus on What You Do Want.
    4:      Facet Truths: Bring Truth Appropriate to the Relationship
    5:      Just Be Polite

ASSERTIVENESS
Moving Forward on Purpose with Respect for Others.
1:    Define Your Win: Values, Goals, and Roles
2:    More Yes/And, Less No/But
3:    Compelling Future: Choose. Plan. Check In
4:    I Have a Point; You May Also Have a Point
5:    Ecology Check

NOBILITY
Royal Knight: Be our highest and best selves.
1:    Leadership: 4P360
2:    Self-Leadership
3:    Chivalry/Bushido
4:    Ladies and Gentlemen
5:    Be a Light, Not a Judge

ALOHA
Love:
1. I want the best for you.
2. I want to be the best for you.
3. I want you to have transcendent joy.
1:    Love Stack: Agape, Phileo, Eros
2:    Love is Not Jealous and Does Not Envy
3:    Phileo Bank Account: Positive On Purpose
4:    Love, Joy, Peace
5:    God, People, Self

PART TWO

OASIS

CHAPTER FOUR

OASIS

Be a Refreshing Refuge.

O-OASIS
H-Harmony
A-Assertiveness
N-Nobility
A-Aloha

The fresh baked chocolate chip cookies didn't actually solve anything – but boy did I feel better.

My mom knew that things were tough, so on that particular day she decided that fresh-baked cookies might help me feel better.

To this day, if I want to feel better, one of the things I still do is bake cookies. I usually find others to share them with since I can't eat that many by myself. I just like the smell of them baking.

Certainly my mom didn't invent the technique. It's so common that real estate agents are trained to have fresh-baked cookies in a home they're showing. So many of us have come home to the fresh-baked cookie smell that we associate it with the best of what "home" is all about.

We call it "life," but, frankly, a lot of "life" really does suck the life out of us. It's like being in a desert. We go through our day-to-day work, our to-do lists, our jobs, our classes, our homework, our tasks, dealing with a mix of nice-people and not-so-nice people… and we need a break.

An oasis, literally, is an area of water and vegetation in the middle of a desert. For those who lived in deserts, knowing the location of an oasis was the difference between living and dying.

Often, life is like a desert. We're out and about in the day-to-day world doing what we must. It can dry out our souls and drain our hearts of strength.

BE A REFRESHING REFUGE

While I was working on this book, an interesting thing happened.

I got a text from a friend who asked if I was available to talk. It was unusual for our contact to be more than casual, so I figured something was going on. We got on the phone and she was in tears.

For the first time in her life, a man had hit her – really hit her – hard. She was shocked, stunned, in physical pain and for the first time she was terrified of a man.

When that happened, she knew one person whom she trusted could help her feel better. Me.

From time to time something like that happens. After all, I'm a martial arts master, so naturally people think of me for protection from violence. What was new was that we were hundreds of miles apart from one another. Obviously, I was too far away to offer any real protection. Yet I had become so associated with feeling safe, that I was her oasis in the middle of that particular fear.

Can I do anything practical from hundreds of miles away? Of course not. It's all emotion. She just felt safer because she heard my voice. That's Oasis.

So you never know in what way you might have an opportunity to make someone's life better. You never know when you might be just the oasis someone needs.

BETTER BECAUSE YOU'RE HERE

The principle of being Oasis is simple: Make it better because you're here.

There are people who walk into a room like a fresh breeze. They show up and it's just better. Maybe it's as simple a thing as a nice smile, that they acknowledge you as a person. It might be a pat on the shoulder as they walk by. It could be something a little more meaningful like a hug or a kiss – depending upon context.

With some people, just their presence is enough. You might not even talk much, or at all, but knowing this particular person is nearby is comforting.

I'm a martial arts master. So, of course, I get to hear some version of "I sure don't want to make you angry!" comment a lot. The truth of it is almost exactly the opposite of that.

I never did find out who she was, but in response to a recent comment on "you could kick my butt," a young woman had something very different to say.

"You're a karate master? Wow. I feel really safe right now."

That was the whole conversation. She kept on with whatever she was doing, and I continued with what I was doing. She felt better knowing that in the room was someone with more than four decades of training to keep people safe. I felt better knowing that at least one person knew they were safer because I was near.

There are too many people you see that require you brace yourself. They might take out a bad day on you. They might be drunk. They might call you names. They might yell at you, judge you, or make demands. The world already has too many of those. We don't need any more.

I've seen a lot of people are exceptional at Oasis. They walk into a room and it just feels like everything will be okay. You know they're on their way over, and you know the problem will be solved. You can face difficulty during the day because you know at the end of the day you get to go home to your partner and get a hug and kiss to end your day.

A colleague had one of the worst nights of his life. He was a performer who had played to sold-out venues many times. He had been out of circulation for a while. He made his triumphant return with a heavily promoted comeback concert at a 500-person venue in San Diego. It turned into a disaster. His refuge that night was his mom. He called her on the phone because he knew that while mom can't fix anything, she can help him feel better.

We can be that kind of mother, father, friend... we can be Oasis for someone.

I AM A REFUGE

Here's the trick of having a Refuge: BE a Refuge.

I've coached people through this process. One of the saddest things I see is when someone demands Oasis, but they don't want to BE Oasis.

It's particularly bad when one person is on offense and gets upset when someone else defends. They want Oasis, they say, but what they really want is a lawful target. They don't want someone to share their day with as much as they want someone to take out their day on. That's not Oasis.

"Make the Relationship a Refuge" means everyone involved is part of the Oasis. It means everyone wins. It means everyone gives. It means people are safe because the place is safe and others are safe to talk to.

It means we seek resolution of differences rather than making others give up what they want so we can have what we want. It means we leave people better off than when they showed up in our lives. And if we can't help them, at least we don't hurt them.

PRACTICAL

Part of Oasis is the practical part. It is as simple as your presence leaves things better than you found them. If you're around, it's easier – easier to endure, easier to do – just easier all around. One of the things I tell the kids is that when they move out, their parents should have more work to do at the house - not less.

I learned that from my mother when I moved out. She had more things to do because I did more work around the house than my presence created. When I left, there was more to do because I was gone. The biggest positive difference from my departure was that groceries lasted a whole lot longer.

OASIS

As part of Ohana, Oasis means your presence makes it better. Your presence makes it safer. Your presence lets someone drop their guard and still be safe. This gives them a place to relax, recharge, and really be a whole person. It gives them a break from that life-sucking desert that life can so often be.

Oasis is refreshing. Oasis is a life-giving refuge.

CHAPTER FIVE

OASIS: WIN/WIN OR NO DEAL

I'm a big-time hugger.

Nancy is a big hugger.

We hugged.

Win-Win!

Yes, sometimes it's as simple as that.

WINNING AND LOSING

We tend to learn about winning and losing playing games. Someone wins. Someone else loses. Some people go so far as to look at anything but first place as losing. Second place is sometimes called "first loser."

Win-Lose thinking comes from a scarcity mentality. We learn it in sports. Because sports are such a big part of our culture, win-lose thinking is constantly being reinforced. In a two-person or two-team game, one wins and one loses. There is only one win-slot, and if one side gets it, the other does not. Wins are scarce. Games are built that way.

Life is more complex. Life is also much more cooperative. Relationships are a huge demonstration of win-win. We both get together, and we both have fun. I get something I want and you get something you want. We're both happy with the outcome. We both win. No one has to lose.

WIN

The "Win" mentality has just one goal: "I win." Many of us are trained to try to win. Many of us are taught to do what we need to do to get what we want and not worry about others. Many of us are taught that winning is our only goal.

I seek what I want. Whether you get what you want it your problem. If you get a win, too, that's okay. If you lose, that's okay, too. If my only focus is that I win, I don't much care what happens on your side. I only care that I get what I want. That's the "Win" mentality.

WIN/LOSE

"Win/Lose" is also common. Many of us are not only trained to win, we are taught to make the other person lose. In fact, some people only feel they won if they made sure the other person lost. Win/Lose thinking is often based in sports or other games.

Doing it as a good sport, you do your job and make sure you're on top. This tends to apply in "zero-sum" situations. Zero-sum is scarcity. If you get it, I don't. If I do, you don't. If we're both after the same job opening, only one of us will get it. The other will not.

Win/Lose with poor sportsmanship can sometimes include sabotaging others. It can include over-winning - pushing hard to maximize the loss to the other person. Gloating may be involved. Trying to crush the other side might be part of the goal.

Win/Lose has a place. There are times there is just one win, like getting that one job or winning the game. A key here is being gracious so win or lose, it's a fun experience for everyone. Even in sports, if it's a good game, even the losers are having fun.

LOSE/LOSE

I see this and it's always horrific. Lose/Lose is when someone does things that destroy what he wants, so he loses. And he makes sure you don't get what you want, so you lose. For Lose/Lose thinking, they only feel they are winning if you're losing. They might actually be losing, but so long as you're losing – or losing more – they're happy. Angry, bitter, vindictive people are often like this.

LOSE/WIN

It may seem unexpected that anyone would go for Lose/Win, but they do! It's the martyr syndrome. It's being a doormat. It's letting others run roughshod over you. It's always being willing to suffer so long as other people get what they want. There are moments when you take a loss intentionally in that moment. As a pattern of behavior Lose/Win is very unhealthy.

WIN/WIN

Win/Win is a much more empowering mentality. I get what I want. You get what you want. We both win.

The more people are winning, the more they want to stay. The more they want to come back. If we have a business deal and we're both happy, then we'll do business again. If we get together for an activity and we're both happy with how it went, we'll get together again.

Win/Win is powerful for any relationship you would like to continue, both business and personal.

Seeking Win/Win can be as simple as finding out what each side wants. Often, one exchange or one event can give everyone what he or she wants.

At a higher level and with more complex situations, get behind the surface desires to the reasons behind what they want. Often, it's possible to find a way for everyone to get what they really want - "the want behind the want."

To do Win/Win well, you need to be able to see things from the other side's perspective. All sides must understand each other. Often we're so focused on trying to make others understand us that we forget to understand them. Most of us were never taught any different, so it must be an intentional practice.

Then we look at what both sides see are key issues. We express our concerns (which is different than expressing our positions). We look at what would be a win for either side and then we get creative in pursuing those wins.

Sometimes, even when we have a Win/Win already, we can look for creative ways to upgrade the wins. When possible, get even bigger Win/Win agreements so we all win even more! That's always a fun adventure!

WIN/WIN OR NO DEAL

A huge part of getting to Win/Win is "Win/Win Or No Deal." We will look for a way for both of us to win, and if there isn't one, we agree to no deal.

I want you to win, just not at the expense of me winning. I will not accept you win, I lose. Likewise, I won't take a win at your expense. If the only way for me to win is for you to lose, then I will not take that deal. I'm not interested in making you lose. I'm also not interested in losing.

One of the most powerful negotiation tools is the ability to walk away. If you can't walk away, then you're stuck with whatever deal the other side willingly gives you. If they do Win/Win, that might work out okay. If they do Win/Lose, that could get very bad very quickly.

Certainly, if you're ever in a situation where the other side cannot walk away, demonstrate Ohana Character by showing up for Win/Win. Imagine the level of trust it engenders when the other side knows you really have them over the barrel, and you're very fair-minded anyway.

As a general rule, if you cannot do Win/Win, then make it No Deal.

CHAPTER SIX

OASIS: GIVE TO GIVERS WHO GIVE

Steve and Rita were separated and had already filed for divorce. According to the divorce agreement, they each kept their car and personal things. They had no joint debt, and they had no assets to divide.

Even though there was no legal requirement he do so, Steve kept giving Rita money. She was preparing to move to live somewhere cheaper. Until she left, her expenses were higher than her income.

So Steve gave her an extra $18,000 during the year between their separation and her departure. Why would a separated ex with no hope of reconciliation do such a thing? Because even though the two of them were ending their relationship, he was a giver, and so was she.

In her case, she was being a great mother to children who had been his stepchildren for years, and even though it was a significant sacrifice for him to do so, he wanted to help make their last months in town comfortable.

He was a giver giving to a giver who gives.

GIVE

Giving comes in many forms.

There are the external things. Some people give money, offering their financial resources in support of churches, causes, or people. Some give things, whether cast off clothing, furniture, or whatever other things they're done with. Charities often receive a great deal of one or the other.

Time is a huge resource because all of us have it, and it is equally scarce for all of us. Rich or poor, we all have the same 24 hours a day. Many of us tend to offer our time or our money to things we believe in. When we apply these things to causes, it's pretty easy to see and measure.

Being giving to people opens us to limitless possibilities. We can be giving with as simple a gesture as a hello and a hug. We can invest our time, our emotional energy, our physical help, and our love in however we do love as a verb. We can offer that which is uniquely us.

In the past two weeks, I've done a lot of giving. I've offered legal advice, business help, personal support, creative services, and practical work. I've given of my time and talents. I've taken calls from crying women, helped navigate complex situations, and helped troubleshoot problems – all woven in to the work that was already mine to do. That's giving.

GIVE TO GIVERS WHO GIVE

The trick of it for me is to give to givers who give. Note that I did not say give to givers who give back. The key isn't that anyone has to give back to me (though, I admit it's nice when they do). It's that they have to give somewhere.

I met one of the crying women as she was giving to others. The other I met at a live-training event and watched the way she willingly shared her talents with others. I've been giving to people I see giving to others.

What they give out isn't very often toward me. That's not my point. My point is to increase the overall giving in the world. By giving to givers who give, I'm filing the emotional coffers of others so they can keep doing what they do.

Meanwhile, there are people who give to me, too. I try to give back when and where I can, but not all giving to me is something I can reciprocate. Often, what I am given cannot be repaid at any level that would be considered fair payment. Certainly when it comes to my mother, all she had given me in my lifetime can never be paid back to her. It can only be paid forward on to others!

Give.

Give to Givers.

From time to time, though, you realize that you're giving to someone who doesn't give. It's easy enough to take note when they aren't giving back to you. In some relationships, there ought to be an easy and natural reciprocation. This is different than a transaction where I do for you and then you owe me, so you do back for me so you no longer owe me.

Reciprocation is when I'm giving to you and you're giving to me and no one is keeping score. Sometimes I give to you more than you give to me. Sometimes you give to me more than I give to you. In the long run there's some kind of very rough approximation of both sides giving to one another. Might it be mismatched? Sure. But if you're not keeping score, you don't care. It's about giving to givers. It's not about some kind of transactional record-keeping on who owes whom for what.

When someone isn't giving back directly to you, that doesn't mean they aren't a giver. They simply might not have something to give that is both valuable to you and suitable for the relationship. If they give elsewhere in other ways, they are a giver. If your giving helps fill their tank to keep them going as they give, you are giving to a giver who gives.

When someone doesn't give back and you don't see them giving elsewhere (except maybe in "you owe me" transactions), it's possible that person is a Taker.

46

The whole quote is this: "Give to Givers who give. Give to Takers only long enough to realize they are Takers, then quietly sift them out of your life."

This may require a little explanation.

QUIETLY SIFT THE TAKERS OUT OF YOUR LIFE

The most obvious way to sift a Taker out of your life is to literally get rid of the person. You might break up a romance, end a friendship, quit a job, or quit volunteering. This is often the most appropriate response to a Taker. There are other options.

When we talked about Givers, we said "Givers who give." If we look at Takers the same way, we're looking at "Takers who take." If you can restructure your relationship so the Taker can no longer take from you, then you have successfully "sifted the Taker out of your life." You've rendered them a "not-Taker" in your life.

By way of example, you might have a friend who keeps borrowing your things and not giving them back. Ending the friendship would get rid of the Taker. You could also establish a new boundary. You could no longer loan this friend anything. This is a way to keep the friend without rewarding the taking.

The Taker might resent no longer being able to take and end the relationship themselves. That's okay. Let them. It shows that they were only friends with you in order to take from you.

If you're stuck in a relationship, some people think it's easier to just keep giving to Takers. The thing to realize is that giving to a known Taker is rewarding them for being a Taker. You get more of what you reward. By giving to someone who just takes, you're going to get them taking more – not just from you, but from others, too. Because people are important to us, we cannot keep "paying" Takers to take.

47

We give to Givers who give. We reward Givers and reinforce giving.

CHAPTER SEVEN

OASIS: BE A SAFE PERSON; CREATE A SAFE PLACE

"The thing I appreciate most about you is that I never feel like you're judging me. That's why I feel like I can really talk to you. I feel safe talking to you."

For people to open up, they have to feel safe. For people to really show up as themselves, they have to be safe. For people to get help, they have to be able admit to those parts of themselves they keep hidden. For someone to feel safe, they have to feel like the truth about them will not result in rejection.

The simple secret is this: Be a Safe Person; Create a Safe Place.

BE A SAFE PERSON

There are many parts to being a Safe Person. The safer you are for people, the more self-evident these will be.

However, many of us were never taught how to be a Safe Person for others. Some of us were specifically trained to pursue popularity or power even if that makes us unsafe. Or maybe we learned to always argue that we're right and feel have to make others wrong. No matter what we learned, we can choose to become a Safe Person.

If it's private, keep it private. This is foundational. It's also just a start. If something is told to you in confidence, keep it confidential. Will there be exceptions? Yes. Those are judgment calls that every individual has to make for himself. Just know that when people realize there's certain information you will not keep secret, they will also decline to reveal that kind of information to you. Be up front about it.

No Gossip. It's gossip when the information being spread will be harmful to someone's reputation, and it's being shared with someone who's not part of the problem or part of the solution. So we only share truth, and if it's private, we share it only with those who need to know. We talk only with people who are part of the problem or part of the solution.

A key gossip principle is this: "He who will gossip to you about others will gossip to others about you." Anyone who gossips reveals themselves to be someone who will share your private stories. That is not a safe person.

No Judgment. Judging someone is saying "you are bad." This is different from "you did something bad." Not judging people means we are slow to draw negative conclusions about people. It means we give the maximum benefit of the doubt that the totality of the facts allow. It also means that we hold loosely to our conclusions even when they are warranted. Some people have epiphanies, and when they do, they sometimes change. When people feel you will not judge them, then they feel safe opening up to you.

No Condemnation. Condemnation is saying, "You are worthless." It's deciding that someone is your inferior. No condemnation means we recognize people's innate worth and our innate equality with them. Even when they have sunk low in life, we recognize how much of life is luck and grace. When people feel they will be valued, they are more willing to be real.

No Negative Humor. Negative humor is giving oneself permission to deliver a negative by wrapping it in a funny.

If you think of a point system, imagine that you get a point for being funny, but you lose four points for being hurtful. What if you do too many of those? You lose too many points and the relationship might not survive. I learned this lesson the hard way as a young teen. I lost a friendship with a wonderful young woman because I learned this lesson too late.

The Past is Never a Weapon. Some people learn to use the past as a weapon to attack someone in the present. These people teach others that whether they are safe in the present or not (usually not), they are unsafe for months, years, or decades to come. To be understood as being safe, we must also avoid using the past as a weapon.

Yes, the past is sometimes relevant. We must exercise wisdom in how we use it. It's often a good tool for understanding. It can be useful for revealing patterns of behavior. How we use the past is another individual judgment call.

CREATE A SAFE PLACE

The Rules Apply to The Place. When we create a Safe Place, all we're doing is applying the Safe Person Rules to a place. It creates a sort of "house rules" that everyone who comes to a group understands.

These rules may or may not always be followed by all members outside the particular place or particular group. That's "Safe Person," and it's up to the individual. However, everyone agrees that if they come here and are part of his group, these are the rules and they follow the rules.

Ohana should be safe. If you ever feel you need a Safe Place and you're not sure if you have it, just start by asking. "Is this a Safe Place? Are we all Safe People? If I'm open, vulnerable, and real, I need to know I'm safe." Just the reminder is often enough for people to willingly follow "Safe Place" rules.

Maintain a Safe Place. Be a part of Safe Place. Even if you don't do Safe Person rules all the time, do it for the Ohana. Do it when requested. If you can't (some people get so emotionally wrapped up in things that they really need to let it out), please excuse yourself so that others can be safe.

THE WORLD IS INNATELY UNSAFE

By unsafe, we do not mean physically dangerous. We mean that there is no guarantee it's safe.

Safe Person rules and Safe Place rules are there so people have their Oasis. There needs to be a Refuge where people can recharge. Be that Safe Person, and be a part of that Safe Place, and as you and others create it, you'll have it for when you need it, too.

CHAPTER EIGHT

OASIS: RESOLVE, CONCEDE, OR COMPROMISE

A significant financial reversal left us paying nearly every spare penny to pay a debt. We both needed a break. We really did. Of all the years we might of needed a vacation, that one was it.

As much as one was needed, that year a vacation was out of the question. With any vacation, all she would think the whole time was "there's no way we can afford to do this." That would just pile on even more stress to both of us.

The goals were in direct conflict.

That year we took a vacation anyway. I found a deal for just $75 that got us a one-bedroom suite for five days. Sure, we had to attend a timeshare presentation, but that put the trip in our budget. We drove there. We used timeshare presentations to get show tickets, and that year we learned a lot about timeshare. Certainly we could not spend our money on one that year, but trading our time for show tickets and meal passes, we ended up having a pretty cool vacation.

The kitchen allowed us to eat for the price of groceries. The presentations let us have some nice shows, at least once nice meal out, and, all in all, a great trip for five days for only about $200. We could afford it, we have a great time, and we learned a lot. (Incidentally, we did eventually buy somewhere, so the visits were legitimate business for the time share companies.)

RESOLVE (MY, YOUR, OUR)

Seek the Higher Third Alternative. Most of us get trained in "compromise," the idea of "meeting in the middle." It's a bit of I win a little and lose a little, and you win a little and lose a little. We'll discuss that later. Higher Third Alternative means we seek an option where you get what you really want and I get what I really want.

I start with My Way; you start with Your Way. When we both have starting positions on anything, we each have our own starting point. If we can let go of the all-too-common feeling "my way is right; not-my-way is wrong," we can look at other ways more objectively. We can look behind our way to figure out why our way is our way. We can consider what our way gets us, and how many other ways we can get what we really want. We can do the same with the other side's way.

My Way, Your Way, and Our Way. The idea with looking behind the My and Your is so we crafted a brand new Our. Our Way is seeking the optimum level of you win and I win. It's taking win/win to the next level. When you want an ongoing relationship with anyone, it's important that both sides be winning.

Highest and Best Win/Win: You're looking for the highest values as you craft win/wins. Resolution means you are fully satisfied that you are getting what you really want, and I am fully satisfied that I am getting what I really want.

It's very powerful to build real Resolution when we began with differences, disagreements or even outright conflict. If we can develop a solution that solves your problem and my problem while making everything better and nothing worse, that's crazy-powerful.

It only takes a few successful attempts at Resolve for both sides to really know that they love and respect one another.

You build Resolve the same way you build Win/Win. You think behind your position to your real values. You explore with your partner for what he or she really wants. What's the want behind the want? What's the win behind the position? How else can it be achieved? Then you keep upgrading to get the highest and best win.

CONCEDE (TRADE WINS)

Sometimes resolution is not possible. Sometimes positions necessarily control. When you try to get behind the starting position, you might not find a higher, better value. This happens when resources are limited. When it's a binary choice between "we either do this with our time or that with our time" or "we do this with our money or that with our money."

When resolution either fails or does not appear to be possible, the second level is Concede. Concede means one of us wins. One of us gets what we want and the other one offers it. The trick to keeping Concede fair and loving is to balance it.

The simple level of balance is that concessions are traded. Sometimes I offer you the win. Sometimes you offer me the win. It's not transactional, though. It's not "it was your turn last time; it's my turn this time" (though you might decide to balance some things that way such as movie-choice or restaurant-choice). It's a general fairness that balances out more-or-less over time. No one keeps score.

A higher level of balance factors in sacrifice and desire. For whom is it a higher cost? Who wants it more? Certainly asking someone to trade concessions that violate responsibilities is always problematic. If only one of you cares, then it's easy to concede to the one who does. Someone who really, really wants a certain food style may consistently get her way over someone who likes everything.

Factor in sacrifice and desire to help define who offers the win. There should still be balanced trading. The danger with letting sacrifice and desire control without trading is that it rewards drama. Most of us would prefer less drama in our relationships.

I offer you a win. This is the trick of Concede. I don't demand I get a win; I offer you a win. Both sides offering shows both sides care. Both sides demanding demonstrates selfishness. Then you both work together for which direction the trade makes the most sense for the relationship.

I accept a win offered to me when it makes sense for the relationship. I should try to be aware of whether I'm getting a disproportionate percentage of the trades. Note that I'm not keeping score to see what I'm owed. I'm looking for where I can give.

Sometimes I might find that I'm getting too many of the trades because when there's a choice to be made, I'm the one that cares. When that's the case, I should go out of my way to find things to give. We call this The Compensate Principle. I compensate for how often I get the win by finding wins to give – or how to make my partner's wins even bigger.

When you know someone is taking a loss for you to have a win, upgrade something else. This isn't a transaction demanded or enforced by them. It's an offer made by the person who is getting their win at someone else's expense.

When you give a win, be fully invested. "Be here now." Be all-in.

This is critical when give a win or accept a compromise. Make sure when you do, do it with a great attitude. If it's something that challenges your attitude, at least make the very best of it.

Focus on the positive. Find what win you can, even if it's just enjoying your partner having a win.

COMPROMISE

I get some; you get some. That's the essence of Compromise.

We go to Compromise when we can't Resolve and when Concede would not be healthy for the relationship. The downside of Compromise is that it rewards overstating one's starting position. Just like Concede can reward drama, Compromise can reward over-stating. Both rely on the other person being respectful of the relationship.

In fact, in compromise-based negotiation, sides are taught to always include things in their initial offer primarily to have things to negotiate away. It's padding the position because you know you're going to go to the middle. It rewards more extreme positions.

I half-win; you half-win. This is what we're after. We want get a partial win/win. When we're Compromising, this is what we're trying to do. When Compromise is going to be the solution, start honestly, evaluate honestly, and give as much of a partial win to both sides as you can.

I half-lose; you half-lose. This is the all-too-frequent result of Compromise. No one is happy. Both sides are upset. For some people, this is the sign of a good Compromise. Maybe when you're opponents, this is true.

When you're partners, both sides should be as happy with the outcome as possible.

CHAPTER NINE

OASIS: LEAVE NO TRACE; BETTER THAN YOU FOUND IT

I was the only high school kid I personally knew who was allowed to have parties while my parents were gone. I'm sure there were others - mostly with more permissive parents. In my case, my friends and I had earned that right.

How did my parents know I had a party? Usually because the house was cleaner than it was when they left.

At the end of the party, my friends would start cleaning. The floors would be swept, the carpet vacuumed, the trash taken out... and for larger parties, the windows and mirrors cleaned, the floors mopped, and more.

So long as my friends kept it up, they were welcome to come over. Combine that with our party-rules and how we enforced those rules, and I was allowed to have parties.

(Basic Party Rules: No drinking, no drugs [or I'll call the police myself], standard Hut Rules, and parents are allowed to pop by any time unannounced.)

LEAVE NO TRACE

Leave No Trace might be best known to campers and hikers. Pack it in; pack it out. Leave nothing but footprints; take nothing but pictures.

The basic idea behind Leave No Trace is to make sure nothing is worse off because you were there. The easy, practical part is to avoid litter. Don't break anything. Pick up after yourself. If you take it out, put it away. If you make a mess, clean it up. Generations ago, these things were common sense.

On a principle-level, we minimize the inconvenience our presence makes to others. We are trouble-shooters, not trouble-makers. We are problem-solvers, not problem-creators.

The Compensate Principle gets used here, too. Sometimes there is no way to literally leave no trace. We might use groceries. Our presence might create costs. Resources might be used on us. We try to compensate for that with balancing contributions. It can be money to offset costs or chores to offset our use of resources.

If we apply the Compensate Principle well, then our presence becomes a net gain rather than a net loss. We can go beyond Leave No Trace to the next level up: Better Than You Found It.

BETTER THAN YOU FOUND IT

Better Than You Found It. Using the camping example, we step it up. Maybe someone else left a trace. We pick up their litter and throw it away. We not only avoid making it worse, we make it better. If there's a lot of trash, we might only pack out a little of it, but it's something.

It might be only a little better, but it's better.

If we and people who think like us show up in enough numbers, we can compensate for the people who make messes. For camping, some people leave trash behind. Enough people like that ruins the wilderness experience for all who follow. By being someone who does more than pick up after themselves, trails and campsites can be kept clean even though some people are not good stewards.

When others create messes, we pick up after them. When others create problems, we solve those problems. When things have gone wrong, we work to make them right. When things are broken, we fix them.

There is a competing principle to avoid rewarding bad behavior. We need to balance being the one that makes things better than we found it with rewarding bad behavior. If a parent always cleans up after a child, the child learns to make messes and leave those messes behind. Always fixing someone else's problem gives them permission to keep creating problems.

This means that we make certain us being around always makes things better.

When there's a problem with someone who makes things worse, we have to deal with that. Sometimes it's not our place. When it's not our place, we leave it alone. We just make things better.

Sometimes it is our place. Sometimes it's not only our place, it's our responsibility. When it is our place we work on positive, Ohana-based means to encourage Ohana in others. Sometimes it's as simple as helping someone see for themselves that they are leaving a mess. That alone is sometimes enough to encourage many people to step up their game.

The principle of Oasis is to make it better because you're there, or at least don't make it worse. We seek to be a refreshing refuge, a person whose presence brings peace, a sense of safety. We seek to be a person whose presence lets others know if we're around, it's better, because we're Ohana.

PART THREE

HARMONY

CHAPTER TEN

HARMONY

Embrace Infinitely Diversity in Infinite Combinations Aimed at Greatness.

O-Oasis
H-HARMONY
A-Assertiveness
N-Nobility
A-Aloha

Marian was invited to Thanksgiving with my family.

She walked in and saw that we were having a huge Thanksgiving party. Lots of familiar faces from the extended ohana from Hawaii were there. She said hello to a few people and headed to the kitchen to see if she could help.

I saw her standing in the entry to the kitchen stunned. She was captivated by... something. I walked over to find out what.

"Look at that!" she remarked. Later she described it as a well-oiled machine, or like a professional sports team, or like a choreographed dance.

In the kitchen were six or eight Hawaiian women miraculously bringing food together. It was the experienced teamwork of women who knew just how to bring this kind of thing together. No one seemed to be giving orders, but everything was happening. Marian was ready to step in to help, but she didn't feel she was good enough to step in at that level of play!

Instead, she joined me and my team to set the table. The way my team came together was that I got out stacks of dishes and people from the party just sort of mysteriously appeared tableside to start setting the table.

Marian had never seen something like that before. To her, it was incredible.

It was an example of Harmony.

HARMONY

Harmony requires difference.

Sameness has great value. Many people find that the more "like me" others are, the easier it is to get along. It's when things are different that getting along is more challenging.

Getting along despite differences is fairly elementary harmony. The simple way is to leave the differences out.

Getting along when many of your views and interests are diametrically opposed is much more advanced. For some people, it's too challenging. Anyone can do it, though. It just takes practice. Like anything else you begin at the elementary level and work your way up.

We see Harmony all the time. In sports, team members play different positions and work toward a unified goal. In music, band members play different instruments and deeply move audiences. In a choir, a collection of voices sings different notes, sometimes-different words, and brings a beautiful song into being.

In a business, a collection of different people work together to make business happen. There are the high profile people and the front-line people we might see, and behind the scenes there are unknown numbers making things happen. Take out any important piece, even if it's invisible, and the whole thing falls apart.

INFINITY

Here's a key idea behind Harmony: Infinity.

When sameness is the only option, all you can do is look for others who are "like me." Similar to sameness is "counterpart." Counterpart is "the other piece" of something. It's the pitcher and the catcher, the quarterback and the receiver, the man and the woman... you get the idea.

When you start looking at differences that come together in harmony, the options and opportunities are infinite. This is how we describe it:

"Embrace Infinite Diversity in Infinite Combinations Aimed at Greatness."

"Embrace" means we take the fact there are differences as a good thing. It's good that we're not all the same. It's good that some of us are good at some things and some of us are good at other things. Note that this does NOT mean that every difference is a good difference. It only means that the fact there are differences is good.

"Infinite Diversity" means there are no limits on how different people might be. Sometimes we notice things like sex, but there are all sorts of ways females do "woman" and males do "man." We may notice race. For some people it's core to their identity, and for some it's incidental. Even when it's core to their identity, what that means also has great diversity. It's the same with religion. Not all Christians agree on all things. If you even split hairs down to an individual congregation, not every member of any given church agrees 100% with every other member of the very same church!

64

Then there's Infinite Diversity in skills, skill sets, education, what books someone has read, social views, values and value hierarchies, life experiences, relationship experiences, opportunities, goals dreams... it's amazing!

"Infinite Combinations" means all these people with all these differences can come together in endless ways. You never know what's possible with the right group of people.

Serendipity is a sort of "happy accident" that can happen when a unique combination creates some wonderful adventure no one would have thought of on purpose!

Synchronicity is when "coincidence" produces a meaningful result. It is nearly impossible to plan either one.

"Aimed at Greatness" is intentional. It's when different people come together with a common aim – something you could call Greatness. This is always positive. It's something worthy. End results benefit many and hurt no one - or as few as possible.

Harmony reminds us that we do not have to be alike to be together.

It's the differences that make things interesting. It's our differences that allow us to form better teams. We can be different and still get along. That's an important part of Ohana.

CHAPTER ELEVEN

HARMONY: DIFFERENCES ARE ISSUES TO NAVIGATE, NOT CAUSES FOR CONDEMNATION

"Wow. Men are amazing!" she said.

Ellen had just then really realized something about men that she didn't really "get" up until that moment. She had been listening to a lesson about how men think and feel about most of the women in their lives. She remembered what it was like being attracted to a man and her challenge focusing on her responsibilities anyway. To learn that men had that kind of attraction to nearly every woman they knew was a revelation.

"How do they handle that?" she wondered out loud. "How do they handle that temptation every single day?" She was honestly impressed. It transformed her relationship not just with her husband, but with every man she knew.

Like many women, she had been taught that men's innate attraction to most women in their lives was a threat. On that day she learned that rather than see it as a threat, to see it as confirmation on how much her man loved her. She learned that this particular difference was proof that her husband chose her, wanted her, and loved her in a powerful, deeply special way.

—

She really got it. She had figured out that the exact thing that lead many women to think men were just jerks and all women were competition was actually proof of his commitment to her. If he felt the same way toward so many women she had felt to that one man who sparked that attraction, it meant that he chose her above all others.

Ellen had successfully navigated a huge difference between men and women. It was not only just a difference (not something broken in men), it was something that both impressed her and made her much more secure in her relationship.

DIFFERENCES ARE JUST DIFFERENCES

People are just different.

To be honest, people are more alike than they are different. We tend to focus on the differences, though. Some of the differences we find wonderful and we are drawn to them. Other differences bother us.

Many differences based upon demographics are what we call statistical differences. That just means they are more likely than not going to be different, not that they are always different. An example is that men are bigger and stronger than women. If you choose a random man and a random woman, the man is likely to be taller and stronger. Clearly, though, there are many women who are taller than many men, and there are women who are physically stronger than many men.

We find differences between people based upon sex, race, national origin, religion, and other large-scale demographics. We also find differences between people based upon individual aptitudes and individual experiences. Differences between people arise even if, on paper, they are nearly identical. Even identical twins with identical genetics and identical demographics are still individuals. As many things as might be the same, every human being is a unique individual.

The better you get to know someone, the more likely you'll run into differences. The closer the relationship, the more probable at least some of those differences can become issues.

DIFFERENCES CAN BE ENRICHING

The first use of differences is to enrich life.

We find out what other people like. We might get introduced to music, movies, foods, and other things that we might not explore on our own. We become more cosmopolitan. We become well rounded.

Many differences are like this. Everything we like now was once new. At one time, it was something different. We were exposed to it, and we found we liked it. Then it became part of us.

DIFFERENES ENHANCE TEAMWORK

Some differences are necessary. Pitchers and catchers need one another. Quarterbacks need centers, receivers, and a whole team of people trying to protect them from being sacked. Highly creative people need highly organized people. We need both warrlors and diplomats.

Even when we don't adopt differences to enrich our own lives, many differences allow us to be more effective as a team. We need people with different aptitudes, temperaments, training and skills.

ISSUES TO NAVIGATE

Then there are the differences that cause problems. These differences are issues to navigate.

If one person is strongly right-wing and another strongly left-wing, that can lead to some toxic political arguments. Considering two of the top political operatives for opposing parties in the country managed to be married to one another, it can be navigated.

Leave It Out. The easiest way to handle a difference that causes problems is to leave it out of the relationship. Just leave it out. Don't talk about it. Don't fight about. Don't make it an issue. You know it's there and you probably won't change the other person's mind, so just leave it alone.

Compensate. Some differences can't be left out. It might be that one person is organized and the other one is messy. The organized person can be responsible for the cleaning. Or the messier person can contain their own mess to their own private area. There are ways to work around it. Use those ways.

Someone Changes. This is only possible sometimes. If someone is going to change, it should be the individual choice of the one changing. It is not to be demanded or imposed by someone else. Some people can learn to be organized. They can acquire skills. They can learn or develop systems and skills to make a change in outcomes even if your underlying temperament remains the same.

NOT CAUSES FOR CONDEMNATION

Many people judge others as bad over what just amounts to differences. They sometimes condemn someone as worthless. Of course, we should not do this to others. We already know we don't want it done to us!

Differences are Issues to Navigate, Not Causes for Condemnation.

Embrace the fact there are differences. Any given difference might be a frustration sometimes. There's a good chance that our differences are equally as frustrating to others at times.

Basic Golden Rule: "What would I want done to me because we're different?"

Differences are a good thing. Not every individual difference is necessarily good. Yes, there are some things that are bad. When there are bad things, those are problems. Problems are there to be solved. That's in the next chapter.

CHAPTER TWELVE

HARMONY: BAD THINGS ARE PROBLEMS TO SOLVE, NOT CAUSES FOR CONDEMNATION

Bob was a thief and a friend. That was an odd combination.

I'm a comic book collector from way back. I have comics in my collection from the 60s, 70s, and 80s. I may not be buying comics these days (despite the popularity of comic book movies), but I have a huge, valuable collection.

Bob was a friend from way, way back. We were all at my mother's house where, at the time, my comic collection was stored. He knew I had a lot of valuable ones in there. When he was left alone, he went in to the collection and stole many of the valuable ones.

What he didn't know was that I knew. I not only knew that he did it, I knew which one's he took. I gave him time to change his mind, but he didn't. He had kleptomaniacal tendencies, and they showed up when desire plus opportunity overlapped – even if it was a friend's things.

I went to his mother's, she showed me to his collection, and I got my comics back. Then we had a talk.

He was one of those friends that the higher the stakes, the more he would come through for you. In the middle of a storm, if lightning struck your roof, he'd be up with you getting a tarp up without any hesitation. If you needed help moving, he was the first volunteer. He had no hesitation to help even when it was a risk or a sacrifice.

But that stealing thing he did… that was wrong. We solved it by never leaving him alone with anything he might possibly want to take. He knew this about himself, so he didn't object to basically having a guard. Other than that, the friendship remained untouched.

The bad thing was a problem to solve and we solved it. Most of the rest of the friendship was good, even exceptional. But bad things are bad things and have to be dealt with.

BAD THINGS ARE BAD THINGS

The first thing to remember about bad things is that they are bad. We're not talking about differences. We're not talking about things we just disagree with. When we say that bad things are bad things we're talking about things that are pretty universally considered bad.

Bob stole. He knew it was bad. He certainly didn't want anyone stealing from him. He wouldn't want other people stealing from people who mattered to him. But he did it anyway. As compulsive as he was about it, he knew it was a bad thing.

SOMETIMES BAD IS SUBJECTIVE

Other bad things are more subjective. Some people think they are bad, and others may disagree. Differences in culture, family background, or even just different values can lead to this kind of disagreement.

It can be difficult convincing someone that something is bad if they don't think it's bad. If that's the case, just leave that part alone. Just go straight to solving the problem. Otherwise you get bogged down in a debate and never get to solve the problem.

PROBLEMS TO SOLVE

Definition of a Problem: Something with a solution.

So many people end up fighting over good and bad and never get to problem solving. It can be just like navigating differences if one of the people doesn't think they're doing anything wrong. You just work out what you need to work out so something isn't damaging the relationship.

If there is agreement over something being bad, it's just a problem to solve. Think about what you did with problems on homework or tests in school. You solved them. That's what they were there for. Problems were there to be solved.

So solve it.

With Bob, the solution was that he was never to be alone with things he might be inclined to steal. If someone's problem is that they have poor control practicing martial arts with junior students, then they only work with senior students.

If someone's problem is that they forget things, the solution would be to make sure no one is relying on their memory. The solution could be a list, reminder notes, someone else reminding them by text, etc. Another is that the forgetful person should never promise anything that depends upon remembering something.

If someone wants to borrow something from me and I'm happy to bring it next time, I don't tell them I will. Instead, I ask them to send me a text or email to remind me before I'm expected to come by. Then if they forget to text me, that's on them. If they do text me, then that reminder helps me. Then I'll put whatever it is in the car right away so it's already there for my next visit.

Problem solved.

NOT CAUSE FOR CONDEMNATION

Even when people do things that are bad, condemnation doesn't solve the problem. If you want them to remember something, calling them names doesn't make them remember. If you want someone to keep doing something you don't like, fighting with them does not build the relationship.

Rather than judge and condemn, solve the problem. At the level of what you consider a bad thing, though, you might need a higher level of adjustment. Some problems can be solved. Some solutions require a change in the relationship. From time to time, some bad things rise to the level that a relationship status needs to be changed.

A martial arts student that makes the occasional mistake and someone gets thumped is okay. Someone that doesn't care that he hurts others is a problem and may need to be removed. It doesn't mean the bad thing makes him a bad person (though it may); it definitely does make him a poor fit.

You might think someone is a wonderful person. That still doesn't make them a good match. If you find that someone does something bad, that bad thing might disqualify that person from certain particular roles in your life. That's okay. Just be friends. Even if you can't be friends, just be polite.

CHAPTER THIRTEEN

HARMONY: MORE FOR, LESS AGAINST: FOCUS ON WHAT YOU DO WANT

He'd go home and yell at his wife and kids. Dan wanted to stop.

My question might have been surprising. "Suppose you stop for coffee on your way home, walk in the door, glare at your daughter and slam the door. Then you pour your coffee over your son's homework and throw the empty cup at your wife when she comes in the room. If you did that, did you yell at anyone?"

"Well…. no." But, of course, that wasn't what he wanted it to look like when he got home. Dan's answer wasn't found in "not yelling." When all he wanted was "not yelling" the only picture that created in his head was yelling.

The trick was to figure out what he DID want. Then he'd know what to DO.

MORE FOR, LESS AGAINST

Mother Teresa was invited to an anti-war rally. She declined. She explained that she wasn't interested in an anti-war rally, though she might be interested in a pro-peace rally.

Most of us are trained to be "against" things. It's far easy to be "against" things than it is to be "for" things. "Against" mostly means you stand up and say you don't like something. "Against" can be saying something is wrong. "Against" can be judging or condemning. "Against" can even just be whining.

The problem with "against" is that you don't actually have to solve anything. All you have to do is complain. Actually solving a problem is next-level-thinking. Proposing solutions and thinking through unintended consequences is much more useful. Some of that begins with figuring out what you are "for."

"More For, Less Against" is "less against," not "no against." That means you may still be "against" from time to time. There are some things where nearly anything is okay so long as it isn't that bad thing. These things might be few and far between, but they do exist.

"More For" means you always look for what you think it should look like. What is the solution to the problem? What is the method to overcome the challenge? How do you craft something so it looks like it should look and does what it should do?

Sometimes it leads you to some surprising conclusions. In my martial art, our goal is to protect and restore peace. That means we want our presence in a potential conflict to be a net-gain for peace. When someone else is being violent, that means that superior force may be necessary to restore peace and prevent evil. We find that to be pro-peace, from time to time, may require force.

I've actually met someone who was "against violence." To her, it was not that evil people used violence; it was that anyone who used violence was evil. To her, and she actually made this argument out loud, that if you use violence to defend yourself against a criminal, you're just as bad as the criminal. If you use violence to protect your children from a criminal, you're just as bad as the criminal. So far, she's the only one I've actually heard make that argument out loud. It is a logical extension of "against" thinking.

Decide what you're FOR. Then Support What You're FOR.

FOCUS ON WHAT YOU DO WANT

Most of us are trained to focus on what we don't want. When we're angry, we argue against something we don't want. When we're afraid, we focus and fret about what we don't want. When something needs to be changed, we tend to focus on that thing we don't want.

Instead, focus on what you do want. Say what you do want. Advocate for what you do want. Ask for what you do want.

For Dan, the answer wasn't in "not yelling." The answer was to decide what he did want it to look like when he went home. He had to think about coming in the door, saying hello and then asking how his kids' day was. Then he had to think about going to his wife, giving her a hug (and not being surprised if she didn't accept it) and saying that he loved her (and not being surprised if she wondered what was wrong).

He created a clear idea in his mind of what he did want it to look like (focusing on his part independent of how anyone responded). Then he paused before he got home to think about, mentally prepare, and then go home. After a while, he could think about it as he drove and start to do it out of habit.

Be FOR things. Think about what you DO want. It makes for much more productive, powerful, and positive discussions. It helps you be Ohana.

CHAPTER FOURTEEN

HARMONY: FACET TRUTHS: BRING TRUTH APPROPRIATE TO THE RELATIONSHIP

"Throw the fight at home."

That was the first piece of relationship advice I received from a professor at my law school. He explained that when you're in law school, you get trained to think legally. You learn how to argue a side whether you believe it or not. You learn how win arguments whether you're right or wrong.

He warned all the incoming law students that it happens over three years and you may not realize how fast it's happening. Your spouse will, though. Your boyfriend or girlfriend will. And chances are high that they won't like it one bit if you use it against them.

Basically, we were told that as we develop into lawyers, leave the lawyers out of our relationship.

FACETS

All of us have many facets to who we are.

Often, facets include all of our roles. I might be an author, a lawyer, a keynote speaker, an executive coach and corporate trainer. These are more job-oriented roles. I might also be a martial arts master, an artist, a romantic, and a philosopher. You could continue to stack roles, traits, demographics, and beliefs in the basket. They would all be true.

You can have more specific facets. I might be a son, but more specifically I am the son of Sheila and the son of Gary, which may be different than "son" generically. Basically anything in you or about you that shows up differently can be distinguished from the other facets.

Each facet likely has a number of truths attached to it that you could consider other facets, too. There might be the part of me that does baby talk and has a certain playfulness with babies. I might not do that with anyone else, but I do it with babies. It's a true part of me, but it only shows up in certain circumstances.

Some facets may only show up based upon relative roles. I am a martial arts instructor, and there are things I will only share with if you are my student. If you are not my student, I do not share those things. This is also often true of parents who understand that a parent has one measure of authority with his own child, but a much more limited measure of authority with anyone else's child.

FACET TRUTHS

The main point of facets is that they should be true.

The more complex and deep someone is, the more facets they might have. There is so much truth there, that by picking and choosing truths to combine, any of us can show up in nearly infinite ways.

I could be hanging out alone, and operate in my demographic position as a person and a man (and all that means to me). Then if I meet up with my wife for lunch at a restaurant, I might also operate as husband and customer. Suppose after that, we meet up with the kids for a movie. Then I also bring father, or specifically father-of-<each kid>, and fan-of-movie or fan-of-genre.

As the facets are mixed and matched, they form new truths. It's a magnificent mosaic that reflects the complexity of all people. The way I am a father to a baby would be different than the way I am a father to a teen. The way I do father at home might be different than how I do father in a movie theater. Same with husband. Certainly how we do husband and wife at home at night by ourselves would include things we would not do out and about in public.

BRING APPROPRIATE TRUTH

Show up with truth that is relevant to your relationships and objectives. Make them true. Do not show up with lies! When you show up with truth, bring the appropriate truth.

If you're with your spouse, show up as husband or wife. Leave the professional at the office and come home as a spouse to your spouse. Same as a parent. Show up as the parent. Show up with all the love, affection, and leadership a parent brings to parenting.

If you're a student, show up as a student. If you're an instructor, show up as an instructor. If I'm at court on your behalf, I'll show up as the lawyer. When I go to my dojo to teach, I show up as the master and the instructor. Where a facet of the truth of me is appropriate, relevant, or even mandated, I show up with that truth.

JUST BECAUSE ITS TRUE DOESN'T MEAN IT BELONGS

The converse is also true. Do not show up with what does not belong. Daddy of a little one probably does not belong in a meeting with a law client. The lawyer probably does not belong in my relationship with a little one. If some true facets of me are negative, toxic, dangerous, or damaged, I would probably leave that part out of all my relationships. That might be things I work on with a therapist or qualified coach.

When our troops return from war, there are trained and developed truths about them that got them home alive. Those truths were the job. They involved tasks and thoughts that are part of war and have little place in civilian life. They did things that make them good at their job, but if they did the same thing as civilians back home, it would be criminal. Returning troops tend to leave those parts of them out of their civilian relationships. Those truths might be shared only with fellow veterans who have similar experiences. They understand that just because something is true does not mean it belongs.

Parents get it, too. There are true things they show up with in marriage, but do not put in front of their children. It's not that they are being dishonest with their children. It's just that some things are inappropriate for those relationships.

There is a context, a place where things are done, a place where things are shared, and outside those places, it is left out because it does not belong in those other places.

For Ohana, you show up with what is appropriate and helpful for building family. You bring the best. You bring what helps. You leave out what hurts. If you need help, you contextualize that, too. Show up with it in a way to get help rather than cause hurt. That's all part of being in Harmony as Ohana.

CHAPTER FIFTEEN

HARMONY: JUST BE POLITE

The disagreement was old. While I set it aside, he never did.

Nonetheless, when I see him, I'm polite. I look out for him. I make sure he has a place, and he's invited to everything he ought to be invited to. As a matter of courtesy, I stay clear of him because I know my presence is an issue for him. It's part of me trying to make it easier on him.

Why? Because there are times it's not about him, and it's not about me. It's about people we both care about. I go out of my way to make sure that's actually true.

It's fairly simple: Just be polite.

BEING POLITE

Being polite is easy for polite people most of the time.

Whether we know all the technical rules or not, if we just make an effort to be nice, most people accept that as polite.

Being polite may include following some or all the rules of etiquette. It may include thank you cards. The basic rule of thank you cards is that if you don't thank the person in person, thank them with a hand-written card. In modern society, even where so much of old-school etiquette has gone by the wayside, hand-written thank you cards for wedding gifts are still considered fundamental.

It can include opening doors for women or anyone, man or woman, carrying a load. It can include remembering to RSVP to invitations so people know if you're coming or not. It can include following the protocol at your martial arts dojo.

ETIQUETTE

There is something called "polite society" that is governed by the rules of etiquette. I've often pulled out my Emily Post book on etiquette when discussing polite society. It's more than 800 pages. It's thicker than my dictionary. Personally, I don't know that anyone actually knows all the rules in it. I certainly don't.

It's a great reference for when in doubt over what's considered proper etiquette. For the most part, the details of the rules are much more than an average person will ever need. When being proper is expected, it's nice to be able to look up what's considered proper. You often discover that much of what is common in modern life violates the rules of etiquette.

For fancier events, it might be worth looking up the rules. We have a tendency to just copy what we've seen. I did. Then I found out after the fact that some of what I copied is considered rude in polite society. I learned the lesson and I did better next time.

For those of us who know the rules, one of the rules of etiquette is to not enforce the rules of etiquette. Basically, if someone is making a reasonable effort to be nice, we take it as polite. If someone is breaking the rules in a way common to society or certain social circles, we accept that it is what it is.

In short, part of polite society is not taking offense at people who break the rules of polite society.

JUST BE POLITE

The better we get at Ohana and more loving, joyful, and peaceful we become as people, the less we'll have ongoing rivalries. As we learn the specific techniques to let go, the fewer issues we'll have with anyone.

Even when these things are true, that does not mean there will be no rivalries and no old hurts.

Even the most mature, most loving, and most forgiving of us will still have issues with some people some of the time. When that's the case, that's when we remember a simple rule: Just Be Polite.

This doesn't mean we have to pretend we like someone. It just means we behave politely. We don't make other people uncomfortable by showing up with our fight when it's not appropriate. We leave the dispute where it belongs – wherever that is.

Maybe it's a legal dispute, in which case we leave it with the lawyers. Maybe we have a personal conflict, in which case we leave it between those involved in the conflict and do not throw it in front of others. We certainly do not disrupt public events or other people's events with our conflict.

We just be polite.

WHEN RIGHT HERE, RIGHT NOW, IS NOT THE TIME OR PLACE

Just be polite just means that you behave in a civilized manner whether you like someone or not. You don't have to like each other to get along.

Be polite just means you extend the usual courtesies to everyone. It doesn't matter if you like the person, you be polite. It doesn't matter if you're in the middle of a conflict, you are still polite. It doesn't matter if you have some old rivalry from some old wrong, real or imagined, and you're still fighting about it. You just be polite.

What it boils down to is that we have to remember what a moment is about. Often, family rivalries create rifts in relationship. They don't like each other and don't talk. When they talk about one another, they complain, accuse, and judge.

Then some family event throws them together. Exes end up in the same room when their adult children get married. Or for a graduation. Or the birth of a grandchild. When these events come up, it's about their child, not them. It would be wrong for them to make it about them and their issues. They need to be there for their child, so when it comes to each other, they should just be polite.

Sometimes we are classmates or co-workers with someone we might normally fight with. Or we end up in a project with someone we don't like or who doesn't like us. Maybe we have a legitimate issue with someone, but right here, right now, is not the time and place for the conflict. So we set it aside for now and just be polite.

For almost all of us almost all the time, just be polite. We can be Ohana and get along even if we have cause to not get along. Why? Because our maturity is bigger than our issue. Because we know that even if there is a time and place for rivalry, we do not disrupt other people's lives over it.

The rule to be polite is fundamental. It keeps conflict out of other people's way. It keeps conflict out of other people's events. It helps protect Ohana in those times we might have some issues we haven't finished resolving. It keeps any unresolved issues between the people who have the problem without pulling others into it.

That can be pretty powerful Ohana. Imagine how great it could be if you knew even if others had a problem with one another, they would not bring it into your event. You could trust that Ohana is bigger than their issue. That's what we're after with just being polite.

PART FOUR
ASSERTIVENESS

CHAPTER SIXTEEN

ASSERTIVENESS

Moving Forward On Purpose with Respect for Others.

O-Oasis
H-Harmony
A-ASSERTIVENESS
N-Nobility
A-Aloha

It was time to make a decision.

Yes, Mark was a friend, but he wasn't getting the job done. The project was falling apart and there was a lot at stake. If this project went bad, it could completely wipe us out.

My emotions ran strong. Anger said to fire Mark since he didn't accomplish what he said he'd accomplish. Fear said to cancel the whole project and run, surrendering the property to the bank and hope we'd survive.

If I was going to be assertive, I had to get centered and make clear-headed decisions. I waited until I was emotionally settled before I went to the property. If my emotions were still high, I'd be more aggressive and less assertive. I admit getting centered on that one took a lot.

I showed up to inspect the project and talk to Mark about where we were. He tried to paint a pretty picture, but when you dug behind the stories, the numbers were clear. We were losing more than seven thousand dollars a month.

This was my measured response. I told him I was putting the property up for sale. I did not know how long it would take to find a buyer. However long that was, to a limit of ninety-days, he could work the project. If he got it to break-even, just break-even, I would take it off the market.

In the months that followed, I helped him with signage, lead generation, and got him a team for property maintenance and upgrade. The work on the property served the dual purpose of helping the project and helping the sale.

Mark's time ran out. In less than 60 days, we got an offer. The project was not at break-even. In fact, he had barely made any headway at all. We set up a long escrow so he'd have time to wrap up and the new owners would have time to set up.

Even then, I showed up in the last couple of weeks of escrow to make sure everything was being cleaned out okay. It wasn't. I got members of other teams to come help and we got done in 72 hours what had been taking Mark a month. The project was done, and Mark and I went our separate ways.

I learned to not get involved in any more projects with Mark. Yet I still consider him a friend. He has exceptional character just as I've known for years. But he lacked the competence for a job like this. Character and competence are two different things. That was an expensive lesson.

He's still a friend. The falling apart of the business partner role is separate from the friend role. I had a decision to make, and he understands that. He was in over his head, and I understand that. I made an assertive decision that looked after higher values, took care of my family, gave him a fair shot, and showed respect to everyone involved.

That is just one way to be assertive.

.

—

MOVE FORWARD ON PURPOSE WITH RESPECT FOR OTHERS

Assertiveness means: Move Forward On Purpose with Respect for Others.

"Move Forward" means you're moving toward something higher and better. It can be as simple as forward movement toward a specific goal. It can be pursuit of a larger mission. It can be more spiritual, the pursuit of some high ideal such as "family" or "love" or "self-respect."

A key to note here is that not everyone will agree on what is "forward." Something called "Miles Law" says: "Where you stand depends upon where you sit." What looks "forward" to one person might not be forward to someone else.

What is "forward" also depends upon one's particular focus. Sometimes things conflict, such as pursuit of career and relationship with family. One may require more time at work, while the other requires more time at home.

This is part of why "on purpose" is also important.

"On Purpose" has two meanings. One is intentional, that you've decided to do it so you're doing it. The second is that there is a higher purpose to it. There are concrete values being pursued or some ideal.

The better we understand what we consider "forward" and what our intended purpose is, the better we can evaluate. When we see what purpose we're fulfilling, we can also understand differing perspectives. For instance, if we're being assertive in our business and career goals, we may realize we're being passive in our family. It helps us live as a whole person more assertively.

"Respect for others" is the biggest difference between "assertive" and "aggressive." Aggressiveness tends to look at people as obstacles, opponents, or tools. Assertive looks at others as whole people who have intrinsic value. It sees that people have their own roles to fulfill and their own goals they are pursuing.

LIVE ASSERTIVELY

We Live Assertively. This means we decide what we choose for life to look like and we pursue that. A great deal of life is driven by circumstances. We must respond. It's just how things go. Even when we are in response-mode, we still get to decide how we choose to respond and how we'll adapt to what is.

Then there also much of life that is entirely up to us. Living Assertively means we take full responsibility and, where we can and should, we take control.

We Learn Assertively. This means we decide what to learn and we learn it. We might decide to learn that which is assigned to us, learning academic subjects, learning jobs, and learning skills for our job.

We can also choose what else to learn, choosing books to read, choosing audios to listen to, choosing seminars to attend, and choosing classes to enroll in.

We Love Assertively. This is often a mind-bender for people who think love should "just happen." It means we learn what love is (we'll discuss it more under Aloha) and we choose to practice it.

ASSERTIVE PRACTICES

We practice Assertive Listening. This means we seek to understand. We'll listen, ask clarifying questions to make sure we understand, and reflect back our understanding. We'll try to understand what someone means by what they say, defining terms, and giving the benefit of the doubt to our communication partner.

We practice Assertive Relationships. This means we learn how relationships work and we invest in them.

The system we often use is the YORI Matrix. The short version is this: YORI stands for You, Others, Relationship, Intimacy. The first place you look is yourself and what you bring to the relationship, then, after that, you look at the other person and what they bring to the relationship. Then you look to the relationship itself, what it is, what it does and should look like, and how this kind of relationship works. If the relationship is more intimate, then you look at that.

YORI also means "trust" which is "I can believe you" and "I can count on you." You do the same YORI sequence with that idea. This is a very brief mention of a powerful relationship system that applies to all sorts of relationships.

We practice Assertive Parenting. There's a lot in parenting that is known. We know babies will need to be fed, clothed, and housed. We know children need to learn language and get their basic education. We know they need to learn to live in civilized society.

Then there's about 20% of parenting that is just chaos. We may not have any answers (which is rough on parents), but we do our best. The more we have a vision for our children that respects who they are as individuals, the easier it is to deal with the chaos. At least we have a starting point!

ASSERTIVENESS

Assertiveness is distinct from aggressiveness. Aggressiveness is "moving without respect for others." Note that it lacks the "forward" since when aggressiveness flows from selfishness, bitterness, or anger, the movement is often not forward. It might be forward, but it might be sideways (it just changes things without making them better or worse), or it might be backwards. Also, there is often no higher purpose. And the respect for others is lacking. In fact, sometimes it's active disrespect for others.

Assertiveness is a virtue. Aggressive is rarely so (some circumstances call for it, but not many). By having cleaner definitions of what we mean, we can Live Life Assertively.

CHAPTER SEVENTEEN

ASSERTIVENESS: DEFINE YOUR WIN: VALUES, GOALS AND ROLES

Suppose I'm on my way home to have dinner with my family.

A violent criminal approaches me. I'm a master of martial arts with 45 years of martial arts training. How do I win?

Well… I was on my home to have dinner with my family. He's approaching me to beat me up and take my money. His win is that he beats me up and gets my money. What's my win?

I get to go home and have dinner with my family.

That's my win.

If I know my win, then I know what to do. I don't have to fight, I just have to get home to have dinner with my family. If I can do that just by leaving before he reaches me, I win. If I have to talk him down so there's no fight, and then I can go home, I win. If he makes me stand up to him and I get him to back off without a serious fight, I win. If it turns into a nasty fight and I have to beat him up, and then I can go home after talking to the police, I win.

But if he comes near me and I pull a "better to be judged by 12 than carried by 6" complete overreaction and beat the tar out of him, and I get arrested and don't get to go home, then I didn't win. I'm in jail. Maybe I beat up the bad guy, but I sure didn't win!

DEFINE YOUR WIN

Define your win. Then you know what you're after.

Defining your win also lets you know when you're winning. You may not have won all the way, yet. If you know what your win is, then you know when you're making progress on your win.

If often remind people "Things are better. Better is good. Better is winning. I like winning." Whether you're winning as fast as you like may be another matter. Whether you're wining as much as you like is also another matter. Winning is good.

There are several ways to define your win.

VALUES

Something that fulfills your values is a win. Something that moves you in that direction is winning.

Your Values come in two basic categories: Moving Toward Values (the things you do want to have), and Moving Away Values (the things you want to avoid). In broad terms most of us want to move toward what brings us pleasure and move away from what causes us pain.

Pleasure and pain are subjective in the Values sense. An intense physical workout can be physically painful, but it gives us pleasure to have a "good workout" because we know it makes us stronger. This is because we value "stronger" and the good workout is how we know we're getting there. The workout may feel painful in the short term, but strong feels more good than a hard workout feels bad.

Values can literally include anything. Values may be as simple and straight forward as valuing Family or Love or Contribution. Or they can be specific. A complete exploration of Values is the subject of a two-day seminar I teach (consolidated to a twelve hour program), so this is barely touching on the subject.

To know your values, just consider what you want and why you want it. Then keep asking why your what or why is important to you. You'll find your basic values quickly. Then look at the choices you actually make. They will show if you have found the values you actually live by. They may be different. We may decide that requires some changes.

GOALS

Achieving a goal is a win. Getting closer to a goal is winning.

Goals come in three basic types: Destinations, Processes, and Compass Headings.

A Destination Goal is what we normally think of as a goal. We're winning when we are getting closer to the outcome we intended to produce.

A Process Goal is a goal to follow a particular process. It's getting ourselves in a regular habit. Maybe it's a habit of exercise, or a habit of reading the Bible, or a habit of training in martial arts. The outcome, whatever it is, will be a natural byproduct of the process followed. This is the goal-based manifestation of "it's about the journey, not the destination."

A Compass Heading Goal is an unachievable goal. Martial arts mastery is like this. There is never a point where I will know everything – ever. That means no matter how good I ever get, I will always be able to look forward to higher and higher levels of insight and mastery. It's a compass heading.

ROLES

Fulfilling a role is a win. When you're getting better it, you're winning.

Our lives are packed with roles. We mentioned these as facets. When you fulfill roles that are important to you, you're winning!

Of course Values, Goals, and Roles all work together. When we fulfill all of it, we're winning. If we know what we mean by winning, we can win more easily. We decide what a win looks like and then we go do it.

Define Your Win. Then win.

CHAPTER EIGHTEEN

ASSERTIVENESS: MORE YES/AND, LESS NO/BUT

I was listening to the boys play a game.

To this day I don't understand the rules (if there are any), but it was some kind of competitive creativity game. Each of the would banter back and forth continually upgrading their idea from something small and modest until whole universes were being destroyed.

Sometimes the theme was comic book characters. Sometimes it was movie characters. Most of the time I have no idea what they were talking about.

The part I kept hearing, though, was "no, no, no...!!!" before they gave their own idea. Each of them felt compelled to invalidate their brother's idea before they gave their own.

I paused to coach them on doing that a bit different. When they learned that when I hear them start with "no, no, no" what I'm hearing is that they don't think their idea can stand with their brother's idea.

If, instead, they said something like "okay... that's good... and now THIS!" it makes it sound like their own idea must be totally awesome.

An approach like that totally shifts the feel of the game. Doing it that way changes a "knock you down so I climb up" competition to "you did well, I'm doing better" standing on the shoulders of giants.

LESS NO/BUT

In the example, it was a couple of boys, a teen and a pre-teen. You expect that from boys that age. You expect it less with grown adults, yet high-powered executives do it, too.

Executives might be in a meeting brainstorming ideas and someone (sometimes all of them) feel compelled to challenge and invalidate ideas as they are presented. That's totally the opposite of what a brainstorming session should be.

Even C-level executives do it in meetings. Someone presents and idea and they feel compelled to find a way to say no, to say but, or to criticize it. They have another idea, maybe even a better idea. Rather than just put their own idea out there side-by-side, it's as though they feel the need to sweep the other idea off the table.

A colleague is in the habit of charging his C-level clients $20 every time they begin a sentence with no, but, or however. He raises tens of thousands of dollars for charity. It sometimes takes the loss of hundreds of dollars during the course of a day for even a powerful leader to realize how often he feels compelled to invalidate.

Even when they agree, sometimes people say "No, I agree." When you agree, it should start with "Yes"! Once more, it's invalidation. It's as though they are saying "You didn't have to tell me that. I'm so smart that I already knew."

Think of all the "no," "but," and "however" invalidations of someone's idea you might hear. If you think about how it feels when someone says no to your idea before offering their own, it's easier to realize. Even if someone compliments your idea, if it's followed by "but," think of how you feel the invalidation of the idea they just complimented.

When you invalidate, think of it as demonstrating the weakness of your idea. After all, if you knew you had a good idea, your idea could stand next to the other idea.

If you have a strong position, your strong position can step up side by side to the existing position. There's no need to invalidate or diminish the other side. Yours is so good that it can stand next to other ideas just fine.

Remember the rule is "Less No/But." It's not "No No/But." There's no need to be militant about it. Make it a guideline and keep getting better.

MORE YES/AND

"Yes, that's a great idea, and here's an another..." has a much more empowering and powerful feel than "No, no, no... I'm thinking..." or "Yes, very good, but..."

As Ohana, one of our jobs is to help others feel empowered. By affirming their good ideas and good positions, we do that. There is no need to diminish others to feel superior.

In fact, "More Yes/And" when everyone in a group practices it creates an upward spiral. I edify you as having a good idea, and I add mine. You affirm mine and add another of yours. Your idea is brilliant, and I have more to add to the mix. In the end, we have a council of great people creating genius.

Yes/And also unleashes creativity. As ideas and positions are left side by side, it promotes listening and good thinking. When an idea is on the table and another idea is added to it, there is the opportunity for both sides to creatively develop absolute genius ideas together. This takes cooperation.

By setting aside the natural competitive spirit of "No/But," we get much better results. No one feels the need to self-judge and self-edit before risking the no/but. That way we get the most creative ideas on the table. That's a powerful way to unleash synergistic, creative genius in any idea-generating or idea-discussing meeting.

So we follow the simple guideline: More Yes/And, Less No/But.

CHAPTER NINETEEN

ASSERTIVENESS: A COMPELLING FUTURE: CHOSE, PLAN, CHECK IN

He got up early in the morning inspired to get to work.

He was engaged and the wedding was coming up. He had a dream, a vision of what he wanted to do for the honeymoon. He would need more money, a lot of creativity, and the wedding would have to be less expensive.

She was all for that. A mutual friend of theirs was a wedding photographer, and he counseled couples to spend less on the wedding and more on the honeymoon. They thought it sounded like a good idea. They still planned the wedding of their dreams, they just looked for less expensive ways to do it.

Day in and day out they both worked a little extra hard to pull it all together. For neither one of them was it a chore. The extra hours of work was inspired by the compelling vision of the wedding and honeymoon.

They found the extra work they did was a joy. Every bit of extra effort brought them closer to that powerful dream of theirs.

THE POWER OF A COMPELLING FUTURE

The power of a future goal is in the present change it inspires.

This young couple had a powerfully motivating goal. They didn't now going in how much of it they might do, but they worked hard at it. Comfortably before their wedding, they had put it all together.

They started with a couple of nights in town as a favorite resort. Then it was off to Hawaii where they had found a deal on a condo a block from the beach. They borrowed a car from family who lived there and bought groceries to eat, saving a lot of money. Then they had a one-week cruise around the islands!

At the end of two weeks in Hawaii, it was back home for laundry, re-packing, and off to Las Vegas for another two weeks. Again they got a condo, ate mostly with groceries to save money, and spent their budget on Las Vegas shows and shopping.

It was an experience of a lifetime, one that would be a memory they could revisit often. Over the years, they encountered difficult times. When life was hard, they could sit and talk about their honeymoon adventure. It helped center them so they could remember the power of a compelling future, and forever have the treasure of a great adventure.

Create a Compelling Future to inspire action.

When you succeed, treasure those memories as a reminder of how powerful you are when you're inspired by such a dream.

PAIN PUSHES

The "Compelling Future" technique is the opposite of what many people are taught to do. Most people learn to make changes by getting fed up with how things are. We're hurt or angry and then we finally make a change. A relationship goes horribly wrong and in a fit of fury, we end it. A job is painful, so we quit. Money is running out so we job hunt.

That's the way so many people learn to do things. People use this system because it works. It's normal. Know this, though, "normal is not always good."

Negative emotions are Emotions of Change. They tell us "something must change." Sometimes those emotions are right. Sometimes they are wrong. Most people use them to make too many decisions, though.

Waiting is a choice. Rather than wait for bad things to drive us, we can decide to be inspired instead. Rather than be pushed by pain, we can choose to be pulled by pleasure.

PLEASURE PULLS

Pleasure pulls. The more pleasure we anticipate, the more inspired we are to do our part.

Think of everything that couple did to put together their honeymoon. It took them months of hard work and creativity, but they were inspired! Think of how hard you work to get ready for anything that excites you.

Remember anything that motivated you because you wanted it, because you thought having it would be fun, pleasurable, exciting, an adventure... and how hard you happily worked to get there. Most of us have at least of few of those, even if we have to reflect on our youth and childhood to find them.

When we're inspired we're enjoying ourselves.

You can decide for yourself if you'd rather spend your life in pain or in pleasure. You can decide if you want to focus on pain to drive and live that day-to-day.

Or you can follow the Create a Compelling Future technique and live life inspired and happy!

CREATE A COMPELLING FUTURE

"Compelling" means it is so inspiring that it gets you up and moving! It is something worth getting up for. It's something worth getting to work on. It motivates you to do whatever it takes.

Some people do this with things like vision boards. They make a poster board or a slide show with pictures or what they want. Often the focus there is material things and experiences. It can also be relationship, spirituality, or anything else that inspires you.

What is important enough to you that it would get you up ready to get started first thing in the morning? What is so much fun that you don't want to stop working toward it? It may be different for each of us, but we all have something that stirs their soul more than anything else.

For me, it's usually experiences with people. I will do more to create an incredible shared experience than nearly anything else. I love planning vacations. It inspires me. What inspires you?

WHAT DO YOU CHOOSE? GOAL.

The basic "What Do You Choose?" is to choose a goal. Having a goal gives you a "forward." Since a key part of Assertiveness is to move forward, you need to know what forward is.

Goals come in three basic types. Each of them is the answer to a different question.

Destination Goal: Where am I going?

This is the classic sort of goal. Think about what an outcome would look like? If there is a "finished product," you have a destination. Visualize that outcome and you know your destination.

Process Goal: What am I doing?

There are times you cannot firmly craft a particular destination, but you can choose actions. If time and energy are an issue, it might be hard to choose a fitness destination, but you might be able to choose a process. You can decide on a course of action and whatever it gets you, it gets you.

This is particularly powerful when you're not sure what's achievable for you. Process Goals can give you the opportunity to try some things and see what outcome they produce for you. Then you can get enough feedback to better craft your Destination Goals.

Some process goals are just habits you want to develop. Religious people might want to develop the habit of reading the Bible and praying every day. There may not be a particular outcome they expect. It's just a spiritual habit they want to acquire. Eating-habit goals, body-care goals, and other shifts to lifestyle are Process Goals. There may be no particular Destination, no "done," just an ongoing process to follow.

Compass Heading Goal: What direction am I going?

A Compass Heading Goal is a direction to go. A classic example is "perfect." It's not a destination. There's not even much of a process you can follow to be perfect. It is a direction, though. Every day you can wake up, look in the direction of "perfect" and know which direction to move.

WHAT IS YOUR PLAN?

How will you move forward? That's your plan.

Sometimes you have no plan. You don't know enough to make a plan. You know what you want, you just don't know how to make it happen. That's totally okay. All that means is that the first step in a plan is "get information." The second part of that plan is "make a plan."

It's okay if your plan is to start off gathering information and then move to actual planning. Just set a schedule for information gathering. You will never know everything about how to do something, so get "enough" information to make a starting plan and start planning.

When you know what to do, just start planning. Once you have a good plan, just get started. Things might go well the first time. It might take adjustments and shifts in direction. That's okay, too.

A key part of planning is this: how will you follow your plan?

For most people, getting information and developing a plan is the easy part. Actually sticking to the plan is the hard part.

You may need a plan to follow your plan. For some people, "just decide" is enough. For most of us, we need more help than that. We may need to post reminders for ourselves. We may need to put things on the calendar. We may need an accountability partner, mentor, coach, or be part of a mastermind.

HOW IS THAT WORKING OUT FOR YOU?

We need to evaluate as we go.

At a basic level, are we doing the plan? If not, then we need to upgrade the plan. We might just need a reminder system, or a better organization system, or help. Many of us forget to ask that basic six-word question: "How much help do I need?" If we need help, we get help.

Since we're talking about Assertiveness, we also look at whether our plan really is a "forward." Sometimes it starts off that way, but as we go, we find that it isn't quite having the impact we expected. Assertiveness also includes "respect for others," and we may find that we need to adjust to show respect.

This is also about Ohana. This is important.

I was working with a financially successful businessman. His business was worth four million dollars. He and his business partner had just split their business in two, each of them individually owning their own company now. Every member of his mastermind group had achieved all of their financial and business goals.

There was a catch. The last of the twelve men was just recently divorced. The men were obsessive about their businesses and finances, and in the process every single one of them lost their family. Wives left them. Kids didn't want to see them.

Ohana-thinking could have saved their families. Maybe four million dollars was a magnificent goal to achieve. Two million dollars and keeping his family together might have been a better goal.

"How is that working out for me?" is the chance to upgrade our goals. We can choose new goals, make them grander, make them smaller, and include more things we might have overlooked.

A key to success in life is testing. We give something a try, see how it's going, take that new information and upgrade our plan. We work out with greater and great insight how we want to craft our lives.

Then we take all that insight to create a compelling future and make that future come to pass.

CHAPTER TWENTY

ASSERTIVENESS: I HAVE A POINT, YOU MAY ALSO HAVE A POINT

A creationist college student finished a biology final early. He and his professor stood out in the hallway having a discussion about evolution. The science professor was braced for all the typical arguments. The conversation didn't go anything like he expected.

"I have a problem with the scientific dishonesty of creationists," the professor said.

"Me, too," the young creationist responded. "I hate that they keep teaching theories they know aren't right just because they don't have anything else. Like hydraulic-sorting for the fossil record. That idea has been falsified because that's not how hydraulic-sorting works. They shouldn't be teaching it."

The professor was surprised. In response, he admitted that evolutionary scientists sometimes play a little fast and loose with the science themselves. In a fairly short conversation, they were both agreeing that real science should triumph. They both agreed that there were holes on both sides.

Then the creationist said "I know there are holes on both sides. I'm just more comfortable with the holes left on the creationist side."

The professor responded, "and I'm more comfortable with the holes on the evolution side. I guess we both hope the holes get filled with more science."

They ended with neither side persuaded, but somehow both sides agreeing. The creationist was still a creationist. The evolutionist was still an evolutionist. Yet somehow they agreed on a whole lot in between and argued about almost nothing.

There was understanding between them, and that was something remarkable. After all, how often do creationists and evolutionist leave a discussion in agreement? How did they do this?

NOT "I'M RIGHT, SO YOU'RE WRONG"

Society tends to teach that if we disagree, it means one of us is right and one of us is wrong. Because of this thinking, we tend to think that anyone who disagrees with us must be wrong.

On some things based upon objective facts, this might be true. If you think George Washington was the first president of the United States and I think it was someone else, then you're right and I'm wrong. If I think 2+2 is 4, and you think it is something else, then yes, I'm right and you're wrong.

An astonishing percentage of life is not like that. With most of life, I will have my reasons for believing the way I do and you will have your reasons for believing as you do.

Remember that Assertiveness includes "forward" and "with respect for others." Trying to prove someone else wrong is only rarely "forward." Attacking someone's position without having a grasp as to their points does not show much respect for others. We can assert a bit of "I think I'm right for these reasons" without having to attack someone else. That's both forward and shows respect.

NOT "YOU'RE WRONG, SO I'M RIGHT."

Worse is the idea that if I can show you're wrong, it somehow shows that I must be right. If you say that 2+2 is 6, yes, you're wrong. But if I say it's 5, I'm also wrong. Showing that you're wrong in no way shows that I'm right. That's not forward, nor does it show respect.

As stated before, most of life isn't a matter of right and wrong. You have your reasons for your position, and I have my reasons for mine.

CERTAINTY SOMEONE IS WRONG IS OFTEN ARROGANT

Arrogance is putting your own thoughts, feelings, or opinions above the truth. There are a lot of applications of that definition, some of them surprising.

The main application here is that when the matter is not simple facts (things you can look up about which there is no reasonable disagreement), there might not be a "wrong" position.

People will often disagree, but if both sides have reasons for their position, then it's a competition between two ideas. Consider Christian theology for a moment. There is one Bible. The books in the Bible are very well established by centuries and centuries of scholarship. The words in the Bible are also established by centuries of scholarship, with very few words or passages that are uncertain.

Does that mean that every Bible scholar, every clergy, every preacher therefore agrees as to what it means? If you were to take a selection of classes from a cross-section of seminaries, would you find that they all agree of all points? Or would you find that many very intelligent scholars, experts in Greek and Hebrew, might still disagree? Of course they disagree! Who's right? God knows. If a position can be backed up allowing the books to be the books and the words to be the words, then maybe, just maybe, it's a right position.

So we respect the possibility that someone who can back up a position just might be right. At the very least, we cannot be 100% certain they are wrong.

Often when others have attacked us for being wrong when we're sure we're right, we presume that they don't know what they're talking about. They might know some stuff, but they certainly don't know everything. We often think that if they took the time to listen to our position and point rather than tell us what they think they are, they might understand better. If they spent a little more effort on trying to understand rather than just fight, they might see our point.

So, of course, we should be respectful enough to do that for others. Otherwise, we, like those who do it to us, are just being aggressive rather than assertive.

I HAVE A POINT

What I can know in all humility and without question is that I have a point. I can know my own position, and I can know how I back up my position. I can know what I believe and the reasons I believe it.

On some things, it's a matter of what questions I'm asking. If I'm asking the question "what belief system can help people live an elevated life?" then a lot of religions might be a right answer to that question. If I'm asking the question "how can I be forgiven by God since I've messed up a lot" there's a much higher chance that I'll find Christianity as the answer. Ask a different question, and different answers become good answers.

My conclusions may also depend upon what assumptions I make. If I presume there is a God because I grew up believing in God, science is not likely going to persuade me that there is no God. If my presumption is that there is no God, it will be almost impossible to convince me that there is a God. There is enough logic and science supporting each side and enough gaps in our knowledge that either side can be rational.

Being able to assert my own position is moving forward. I have a known position that I back up with points (information, logic, principles, etc.). That's a particular forward, a bit of supporting what I'm for rather than arguing what I'm against. If I'm not saying someone else is wrong, I'm just discussing the rationale of why I hold my position, then that's showing respect.

YOU MAY ALSO HAVE A POINT

All the same things apply in the other direction. I cannot know if someone else can support their position if I am unwilling to hear them out. If I assume they have a point, then I can ask. I can find out their position and how they support their position. Likewise, their conclusions might depend upon their questions or their assumptions.

This also invokes what we call the Law of Reciprocity. If I argue, you argue. That's a fairly natural reflex. If I listen, you listen – another fairly natural reflex. Some people never learn, so it's not 100%, of course. Some people are just aggressive. When you're respectful, though, they look aggressive. When you respond with aggression, it just looks like a debate or argument.

The Law of Reciprocity is a powerful principle. We see it in successful businesses all the time. In sales, they use it to persuade to the initial purchase. Great customer service provides great service values as the reciprocal of the initial purchase. Great action tends to produce great reactions.

THE GOLDEN RULE

Treat others the way you want to be treated. We all know this basic, simple, almost self-evident life-rule. We want others to consider the possibility that maybe we're right. Even if they disagree, we want them to see that maybe we have a valid point. If that's what we want from others, then we should do the same. We need to consider that people with whom we disagree might be right, that they might have a point.

If I listen to you, the Law of Reciprocity says that you should also listen to me. On the other hand, if all I do is argue with you, reflexive reaction will tend to have you either just arguing with me or disengaging and not discussing it at all. Either way, I don't actually persuade anyone of anything. It's better if both sides listen.

Since the Golden Rule is to treat others the way you want to be treated, you do it even if the other person does not reciprocate. It's not "treat others the way they treat you." Leaders go first. We do it right first. We try to show others how to do it by example and explanation. When we've modeled it enough, we can talk about it. Even if that individual doesn't ever come around, others will see that we really do what we say we do. If we can remain assertive in the face of aggression, that commitment increases our credibility.

I HAVE A POINT; YOU MAY ALSO HAVE A POINT

"I have a point; you may also have a point" also has the curious power of making you "never wrong." After all, the only way you could be "proven wrong" is if someone can prove that you really don't have a point at all.

If they argue that they are right and you are wrong, remind them that all you're arguing is that you have a point, that you have reasons you believe as you believe. They may disagree with your position or your belief, but all you are asserting is that you have a reason for your position.

By respecting the fact that you believe what you believe for your reasons, and I believe what I believe for my reasons, we can talk about it. We can talk about your reasons. We can talk about my reasons.

If I understand your reasons better, I might be persuaded. If you understand my reasons better, you might be persuaded. Even if no one is persuaded, at least we understand one another better and respect one another more – and that is great progress!

It also requires that I get better at being assertive. I have to learn my own position better so I can explain it. I have to understand your position better so I can effectively deal with the questions your reasonable position might raise about my position. It's good for me. It helps me with my "forward," and it gives me a forum for showing I have respect for others.

It's a win all around. It's powerful for building and sustaining Ohana even when we disagree.

CHAPTER TWENTY-ONE

ASSERTIVENESS: ECOLOGY CHECK

An "Ecology Check" is a simple, three-question check to see if something is a good idea (or at least not a bad idea). The questions are very straightforward:

1. Is it good for me?
2. Is it good for others?
3. Is it good for the world?

The answers to these three questions tell you if what you're doing or planning is "forward." It helps you consider if it shows "respect for others."

IS IT GOOD FOR ME?

Is it good for me (or at least not harmful to me)?

Obviously, if something is outright bad for you, don't do it. At the very least, if you're doing something you know is unhealthy, compensate for it in some way. If you know you've made a choice that causes stress, can you build in a stress-reliever? If you know you've made a choice that puts you in danger, can you have safety protocols to limit the danger?

Because of responsibilities for others, some people forget to take care of themselves. In particular, mothers have a reputation for this. Even if you have a very good reason to be pushing yourself hard, you need to take care of yourself. If love and responsibilities require that you push hard, find a way to compensate. You need to find a place to get filled so you don't run yourself down to empty. You must find a way to fill your tank so you can do the things that are yours to do.

By including enough things that are good for you to compensate for anything that might be harmful (even if for very good reason), you can keep going much more effectively.

IS IT GOOD FOR OTHERS?

Is it good for others (or at least not harmful to anyone)?

We should always be making an effort to help rather than harm. Yes, sometimes there is a difference of opinion on what is good for someone. Tough love often lands in this disputed territory. Certainly what some consider co-dependent does. Whatever we do, we should always make our own best effort to make sure what we do is good for others – or at least not harmful to anyone.

IS IT GOOD FOR THE WORLD?

Is it good for the world (or at least not harmful to the world)?

Most day-to-day activities have negligible impact on the world around us. Thus those things would fall into the "at least not harmful to the world" category. Where what we do does have a larger impact, is it helping or hurting?

THE THREE-QUESTION CHECK

The three-question Ecology Check is a simple, easy way to look at any decision we're considering. The more it's good, the more likely it's a good decision. The more it's harmful, the more likely it's a bad decision.

Of course there are many other factors involved. It might be good for some people and bad for others. It might be good in the short-term but harmful in the long-term, or the other way around. It might be good for the world in one way, but bad for the world in another way.

As simple as the three-question check is, yes, the answers might not always be as clean as a simple good/bad decision. However, when something isn't clearly good, it does inspire us to take another look at our options.

A BETTER WAY

A big insight on the Ecology Check is to see if there is a better way. Suppose I find that an action is good for me, harmful to some others, and does not impact the world. Is there a slightly different way I could do the same thing that would eliminate the harm to others?

Always look for a good way. Sometimes, even if you have a good way, you might find there's a better way. Maybe you can mitigate the harm to others or to the world, making it less-bad even if you can't make it good. Sometimes you have to look at the Big Picture and consider the good/bad balance of your alternatives, or the good/bad of not making a decision.

Ultimately, the goal with the ecology check is to find the overall best way available to you. You're seeking the way that is the least bad and most good on each of the three questions. Just asking the questions can prompt thought.

Knowing you have the best answer you could find or develop provides peace. When you know this really is good, or as good as you can manage, it allows you to move forward with greater certainty that you've made a good decision.

PART FIVE

NOBILITY

CHAPTER TWENTY-TWO

NOBILITY

Royal Knight: Be our highest and best selves.

O-Oasis
H-Harmony
A-Assertiveness
N-NOBILITY
A-Aloha

I lived at home and attended a university I could see from my bedroom window. My friends had gathered for our weekly game time. There were six of us hanging out downstairs at my mother's house.

We were into our game when my mother came downstairs. "I need help!" she said. "One of the neighbor ladies up the street had a pipe burst, her husband is out of town, and we need help up there!"

The team of six young men instantly mobilized. We headed up the street with my mother to the house of a woman none of us had ever met. The water had already been turned off, so it was mostly heavy lifting and cleaning up water. In a couple of hours we had everything off the floor, most of it outside, the water cleaned up, and everything was safe – for now.

She would still need to call a plumber to fix the burst pipe and a service to come dry out her carpets and see to her walls, but the immediate problem was handled. None of us knew her. To these six young men she was simply a damsel in distress, a lady my mother's age, and she needed help.

For these six young men, it felt a little extra cool that we were helping a lady. To be honest, though, we would have helped anyone. That's what we did.

That's how this particular group of friends operated. Some people wonder where such young men and women are today. Frankly, I see them all the time everywhere. I see it in men and women, in young and old, and across all demographics.

It's much more common than we sometimes realize.

KNIGHT IN SHINING ARMOR

The "knight in shining armor" ideal reminds us to face life with the courage of a knight heading toward battle. Problems, challenges, and crises are dragons to be slain. Goals are treasures to be won.

Sometimes it shows up in ways very much related to potential combat.

They heard a woman screaming. Two young men and a young woman headed out from to see where it was coming from. It was near. A man was yelling. A door slammed hard, and it got quiet. Then they heard her crying.

They went to the house with all the noise and heard the cries at a window on the side. The layout was just like another house they knew, so they got near that window and could tell that a woman was there by herself. They asked if everything was okay. She said no. She asked if they could call the police. She was safe for now, but she really wanted the police there before he came anywhere near her again.

The three neighbors called the police. Then they lingered nearby out of line-of-sight from the house. They had a plan to go in to help her only if there was immediate danger. One of them would engage the man and try to calm things down. The young woman would get the woman to safety. The third would be the buffer in between.

Fortunately, as hoped for and expected, the police arrived. Everyone relaxed. They acted wisely. They were prepared to act bravely. That's knightliness.

That is particularly important to me because my very first contact with death was the murder of a family friend. She was heard screaming for help in the middle of the night. No one came. No one so much as called the police. The killer was never found.

You can imagine I appreciate those with the level of knightliness to be ready and willing to help. I likewise appreciate the wise restraint shown so they did not escalate the situation. I wish my friend would have had neighbors like that.

ROYAL KNIGHT

The ideals of the Royal Knight blend royalty with knightliness.

"Princess" sometimes has competing meanings. Some take it as an entitled, self-absorbed, demanding woman. Of course, that's not what we mean here. Others take it as something wonderful. Obviously that's what we mean.

We draw on the definition of Ohana popularized by Disney. We also draw on the Disney-style princess. Think about them. There's beauty, grace, and kindness in the classic princesses. There are the smarts of Belle, the courage of Mulan, and the resilience of Pocahontas. Of course there are the kind of limitations and stereotypes you'd expect in a children's movie, but each princess has virtue and we focus there.

We have precious few popular Prince characters to draw upon for specific examples. They tend to be more two-dimensional than the women, but they are routinely brave, willing to risk for what's right, for duty, and for love.

For our purposes, royalty is also about leadership. It's about taking responsibility to be a leader. The more you learn about the leadership system 4P360, the more you realize that you are a leader everywhere. The average person touches the lives of 20,000 people over the course of a lifetime. Whether a moment with a cashier, or a lifelong relationship with family or friends, how we touch those lives means something.

121

Knightliness combines modern concepts of chivalry and the samurai concept of bushido. It's about courtesy, fairness, and courage. It's about being a gentleman or a lady, and knowing when it's important to do it and when it is best set aside. Diving in to both chivalry and bushido as it applies today is a powerful metaphor for living.

HIGHEST AND BEST SELF

"Highest and Best Self" is self-evident for some people and a confusing concept for others.

Consider that one of the highest ideals in life is love. When you feel love for others, when it's really powerful, when love overflows your heart, what does it look like in you? The kind of love you might feel early in a romance often inspires great things in us. The kind of love we have at engagement or marriage also does it. So does that moment when we first fall in love with our newborn child. Almost universally, that bright, shining, glowing feeling of love inspires us to our highest and best selves.

Another high ideal is joy. Yes, it's true that many people do all sorts of "not so high and not so best" things in pursuit of pleasure or happiness. But think about the other side of that. What do we do when we're at our happiest? What do we do when we're most joyful? When that special kind of happiness bubbles up from somewhere within, what are we like? When we're already happy, what do we do? That's often from our highest and best self.

Think of what kind of person you are when you're at your most peaceful. When you feel most centered. When life feels in balance. Think about where you are in life in those moments of abundance. When you feel like there's plenty for everyone and a lot of it is coming to you, what are you like?

Most of us get an idea of our highest and best self somewhere in these examples, maybe in all of them. The goal is to bring that person to our Ohana as often as possible.

CHAPTER TWENTY-THREE

NOBILITY: LEADERSHIP: 4P360

Being the boss who likes people and hates to give bad news makes firing someone particularly hard. Andy was such a boss.

He had to fire someone. Because he hated to do it, he kept the poor guy waiting in the lounge for hours. I had a meeting with Andy, and I saw the gentleman sitting patiently waiting for his meeting. He knew what was coming. It was just a question of how long he would wait before it actually happened.

Andy was still in the early stages of learning 360-degree leadership. That was the day I taught him how to do something terribly negative, like firing someone, in a positive way. I told him I would fire this man for him.

We invited him in, asked about what he thought of his job performance, and he readily admitted that he wasn't able to do his job. He had a good reason, but he was on a four-man team that was idled every time he was late or couldn't make it in. He asked if he was being fired.

I told him that if there was a reason he would prefer to be fired, we could do that. If he would rather resign on the basis that he was not able to do the job, we would accept his resignation. We also told him that if he would show any future employer the courtesy of taking responsibility for whether or not he could do a job, we would give him a great recommendation. After all, we thought he was a good guy who did good work, but his life just wasn't good for the four-man team system we used.

He understood. He shook our hands with a thank you. We did give him a good recommendation. The basis was that our experience with him was that when he could not fulfill what we needed from him, he took responsibility. We separated amicably. Our understanding was that he learned a valuable lesson that helped him in his next position where he was very successful.

It took what might often be devastating and made it a mini-seminar that helped him succeed. 4P360 Leadership turned a negative experience into a positive one.

4P360 LEADERSHIP BASICS

4P360 stands for 4 Pillars, 360 Degrees. It comes with Four Pillars, Four Rules, and Seven Directions. Two of the directions are called Zero Point Leadership. The metaphor is "Double 0 Seven" to help you remember there are seven directions, and two of them are called "zero point leadership."

This leadership system is simple enough to get the basics in one short chapter. It is sophisticated enough that you could invest decades truly mastering it. Here's the introduction to the four pillars, the four rules, and the seven directions.

FOUR PILLARS

Powerful. This simply means whatever you do must work. Too often, this is as far as many leaders go when they think about what they're doing.

Practical. This means it should be a technique that could be made policy without causing unintended negative consequences.

Principled. This means what you do should work on larger principles, "big rules," so that they may be adapted to other specific situations. The principles being used should be able to be consistently applied. Then they must actually be applied consistently.

Positive. This is often overlooked when it comes to troubleshooting. Even very negative situations, such as firing someone, can be done in a positive way if you know how. If even negative situations are handled in a positive way, everyone will have greater trust that they will be treated with dignity no matter what happens.

FOUR RULES

Copper. Think through it. We have several examples in the business world. Nordstrom's employee policy "use your own good judgment." IBM's "think." Apple's "think differently." If we step back from the emotion, look at a situation, and think through it before we act (and apply the four pillars and four rules), it's amazing the quality of decisions we can make.

Silver. Do no harm. That which you hate, do not do. Or to match typical Golden Rule language: Do not treat others the way you do not want to be treated.

Gold. We all know the Golden Rule. Treat others the way you want to be treated. You often hear the King James-style language: Do unto others as you would have others do unto you.

Platinum. Treat others the way they want to be treated. This is the actual meaning of the Golden Rule clarified here for those who might choose to misinterpret it.

SEVEN DIRECTIONS

Down. This is what we conventionally think of as leadership: leading from in charge to those who are subordinate to you. Of course, this is indeed leadership. In 360-degree leadership, it is barely the beginning, though.

Up. Leading up is leading those to whom you are subordinate. Leadership is influence. Leadership is making a difference. Leadership is handling your job well without your boss having to directly supervise. Leadership is being a good example. In all these ways, your presence can change the behavior of those to whom you report, especially if you understand this essential leadership skill.

Across. This is leading someone when neither of you is in a line of authority to one another. It's influencing peers.

Diagonal Down. This is leadership influence with those who report to your peer or are peers to your subordinate. The extra bit of sophistication here is that while you are influencing an outcome, you do so with respect for the other relationships involved. You want to protect the authority relationship the person or department has with your peer and the peer relationship they have with your subordinate.

Diagonal Up. This is leading the peer of your superior or the superior of your peer. It has additional importance because if it handled poorly, it can impact how that leader interacts with your peer or your leader.

ZERO POINT LEADERSHIP

Self-Leadership. This is leading yourself. This is actually the hardest leadership to do. It's also the most important. It is the subject of it's own chapter.

Reverse Leadership. This is teaching others how to lead you. Whatever you let work you are teaching works on you. Whatever you do not let work you are teaching others won't work with you. By setting easy-to-follow and effective ways to influence you, you are training those around you to treat you a certain way.

CHAPTER TWENTY-FOUR

NOBILITY: SELF-LEADERSHIP

I watched her follow the program all by herself. She wasn't part of a group. She didn't have someone looking over her shoulder. She didn't have a life coach. Marie just decided to seriously upgrade her health and fitness, so she did.

It was a three-week program and she stuck to it. I was impressed. In three weeks, her skin was noticeably clearer, her eyes shined brighter, and her energy levels were up. She dropped ten pounds in those weeks.

Then she started another program, a 90-day workout program. She followed with another 60-day program, and then another. No one made her do it. She just did it.

Over the age of 50, and she was in better health than ever before in her life. Her fitness levels rivaled her high school years when she was the most awarded student in her school.

She kept up her new behavior for months until it became a new habit. Years later, she's still at it. It's easy for her now. Now, it's become part of who she is.

To get there, though, she had to lead the hardest person to lead: herself.

WHY WE'RE THE HARDEST PERSON TO LEAD

Two percent.

That's just one-in-fifty. One-in-fifty people excel at self-leadership.

Why would this be?

Think about any time your leader asks you to do something. You have to do it because it's your job. Someone with the authority to tell you what to do has told you what to do so you do it.

If someone without authority asks something of you and you agreed, you do it because you said you'd do it. You keep your promise because you promised. You do what you said you'd do because you said you would.

What if you wanted out? If you wanted out of something the right away, you'd ask to be released. You'd ask your leader, ask your friend, or ask whomever it was you made the agreement with.

If they willingly release you, then you're off the hook. You don't have to do it because the person you promised said you don't have to.

Here's our self-leadership problem: If I want to be let off the hook on a self-leadership thing, whom do I ask? Me! If I want out, and I have to check in with myself to see if the me that wants out will let me out. Of course I'll give myself permission!

Imagine if every time you went to a leader or a friend to ask to be let off the hook on something, not only were they willing to let you go, they actually really wanted! Imagine going to your boss, and your boss now wanted you to not do it. Imagine you go to your friend, and your friend now wanted you to not do what you said you'd do. Not only would you be off the hook, but no one would be upset!

That's the problem with self-leadership. We follow the same rules we follow with other leaders. Except when we are leading ourselves, we have to play both roles. We have to look at it from two different perspectives at the same time.

SELF-LEADERSHIP: HOLDING TWO ROLES

I get in trouble when I try to lead myself from just one role. If I'm just Scot leading Scot, then when Scot decides to do something and Scot later doesn't want to do it, Scot will let him off the hook.

The trick is to hold two roles simultaneously.

Assume I'm being a responsible leader and I've asked someone to do something that they ought to do. If they later come to me and ask to be released, how will I make that decision? Will "I don't feel like it" be reason enough? Of course not. There would have to be a good reason.

By holding the role of "responsible leader" separate from "me" I can make better leadership decisions for my number-one follower – me.

MAKING THE LEADER CHOICE SEPARATE FROM OUR EMOTIONS

The Responsible Leader is a role based on responsibility rather than emotion. Think of it as the adult-self, or a more grown-up, mature, wiser self.

Commonly, people make choices emotionally and justify them logically or philosophically. Part of our job is to separate ourselves a bit from our emotions and make leadership-decisions for ourselves. If I were an executive coach, and the executive was similarly situated, what advice would I give? What would I think would be the best thing to do? That's the kind of decisions I want to be making for myself. I am the executive in my own life.

Leadership should be powerful, so it must work, which means however we make choices must work or it's not good leadership. This is the biggest problem we have with self-leadership – making it work.

Practical, principled, and positive are also key parts to self-leadership. We need to think it through and consider whether we think it would be a good idea to let someone else off the hook. If not, then we don't let ourselves off the hook. We actually want to stop and think about it. That's basic Copper Rule: Think Through It.

Then we follow through on what we decide is best – no matter what we feel.

CHAPTER TWENTY-FIVE

NOBILITY: CHIVALRY/BUSHIDO

"You're here. Now I know we're safe."

Something black belts get all the time is "I better not make you angry!" That might be true for someone who is just a fighter. It might be true for someone who is dangerous for any reason. For a true martial artist, though, for someone who has any kind of warrior code, that code-governed person is the safest one to make angry.

Instead, as a very pleasant surprise, Annie, upon being introduced to me as a martial arts master, remarked, "You're here. Now I know we're safe." She understood that when someone is highly trained and also has a code, people are safer in their presence.

With a code, power is used to protect. That kind of code, a code of chivalry, a code of bushido, or any of many warrior-codes, help us live an elevated life. It makes the presence of a warrior welcome, because such warriors are not threats – they are peacemakers.

MODERN CHIVALRY

When we think of modern chivalry, we tend to think of gentlemen treating women like ladies. That's certainly part of it, and that will be the topic of the next chapter. Here, we're exploring chivalry in a bit more of a classical sense. Then we're adapting it to modern needs.

At the highest level, classical chivalry included Duty to God. The ideals here included being a champion of good against evil, protecting the innocent, defending the defenseless, and being generous.

Next in line is Duty to Others, starting with one's lord, one's military peers, and then fellow citizens and all Christians (which we can think of as those whose values you may share no matter where they're from). As with Duty to God, it includes protecting the innocent and defending the defenseless. It also includes mercy, courage, heroism, and fairness.

Finally is Duty to Women. This is unusual in that chivalry provides additional responsibilities when it comes to women specifically, perhaps, in part, because warriors-without-a-code are historically notorious for brutality against women. The extra duties to women that extend above and beyond the generic duties to all people sets a high value on women, a reminder for the strong, hardened warrior to be gentle and gracious. The modern equivalent is for men to be gentlemen and women to be ladies, understanding how much and when to do so, and to do so from a place of mutual respect and honor.

THE SAMURAI CODE

The Code of the Samurai is very similar. Historically, it was a little fuzzy, as was chivalry. It did coalesce into a list of seven classical virtues. These help us consider how these historic traits can help us live an elevated life today.

GI (HONESTY)

Gi (Honesty) - Seek, speak and live by what is true. Related to this is one of our core values: Reality is more important than anything we believe. First, we look for what is true, speak only truth (which means we're careful with our vocabulary), and do our best to live by truth. We're open-minded enough to understand that because we don't know everything, what we believe is subject to adjustment as we learn more. We correct ourselves as we learn more.

YU (COURAGE)

Yu (Courage) - Fear touches the heart of all who must stand for what they hold dear, but what is important is that the samurai stands above his emotion. Courage means "I feel fear; I'm going anyway." Courage is recognition that emotions should not control our lives. There are values higher than how we might feel in the moment, whether fear, anger, hurt or hopelessness. It is a manifestation of Willpower: I will stick to what is right no matter what I feel.

JIN (COMPASSION)

Jin (Compassion) - A truly wise person tempers the power he holds over others with compassion for them. We apply the Golden Rule. The first level of spirituality is recognizing the innate value of others. The phrase "there but for the grace of God, go I" reminds us that we or others we love could have been on the other side of anything we're doing. We make our choices accordingly.

REI (COURTESY)

Rei (Courtesy) - A sword does not make a samurai, but it can unmake him. Through courtesy, one may create peace. This is a fundamental of all warrior codes: the idea that the ability to fight can destroy everything the warrior is pledged to protect unless governed by a code. Fundamentally, that code is grounded in courtesy. In some contexts, it can be called professionalism. In our martial art, the protocols are our rules of etiquette. Whether someone is friend or foe, you're still polite. As rei (courtesy) reminds us, "through courtesy, one may create peace." This applies in personal relationships with partners every bit as much or more than with strangers or opponents.

MEYO (HONOR)

Meyo (Honor) - Do the right thing. While this word sometimes gets abused (bad guys claiming to have been "dishonored" for having their cheating revealed, for instance), it's a good word. Fundamentally, it is "do the right thing." If we apply the principles of 4P360 Leadership (earlier chapter), we can sort out what's right.

Our second core value helps us: All principles must be consistently applied. If others used the same idea of "right thing" as we are, would that be a good thing? If we look at the ecology check (discussed under Assertiveness), that helps us figure out the right thing. Yes, sometimes right and wrong might seem a little fuzzy and we have to make judgment calls. Most of the time, though, it's pretty clear.

MAKOTO (SINCERITY)

Makoto (Sincerity) - Mean what you say, and if you do not mean it, do not say it. This concept can be a particularly deep. There are some things we say because they are true even if we do not feel them in the moment. For example, it may always be true that I love my wife, but in the moment I might be angry because she's doing something I dislike. Does anger mean I don't love her? Of course I still love her. I'm just not feeling it at the time. I'll still say the words "I love you" because those words are still true.

Makoto says, then, that I should mean it when I say it. I do mean it, always, in the sense that it's true and I know it's true. Because it's true, and I'm going to say it because it's true, I should also mean it emotionally. That means I need to shift my focus to my love for her in that moment I'm speaking that truth. That, in turn, helps me settle in to that love so we can be more effective in solving whatever the problem is that might have triggered my (or our) anger.

The same applies to movement. In martial arts, we practice movements that are intended to have a particular effect. We execute the movement with a focus on moving as to produce that effect. Do what you intend to do, and do it like you intend to do it. This simple idea could be applied to a thing as simple as having agreed to go shopping with my wife. I go like I intend to really be there enjoying shopping with her. That's part of makoto, too.

CHUGO (DUTY)

Chugo (Duty) - Everything serves something, and even the greatest Emperor must bow before Heaven. We've talked about duty under chivalry as Duty to God, Duty to Others, and Duty to Women. This can also include obedience to the rules, whether we're talking about the rules at a dojo, a business, someone's home, or the laws of a city, state and nation.

LIVING BY A CODE

Books can and have been written about chivalry, bushido, and other codes. Many warrior groups and cultures have had their own version of a code through the ages. The more powerful someone is, the more important it is to have a code to govern the use of that power.

History shows us the great peace and stability that can be brought about by great power under great control. We also have abundant examples of what can happen when there is power wielded without a proper code to govern the use of that power, or when the code is ignored.

For Ohana, we have our code, too: Oasis, Harmony, Assertiveness, Nobility, and Aloha. As with all codes, we can then dive deeper into each aspect and think more profoundly about how to use each aspect to live an elevated life. As illustrated here, even a deep dive will never fully exhaust the philosophical considerations we might ponder. As ever, though, we keep the fundamentals in mind: we are seeking to live an elevated life. We are seeking to be Ohana.

CHAPTER TWENTY-SIX

NOBILITY: LADIES AND GENTLEMEN

He was really, really angry.

As he and his mother left the dojo, we watched as he stomped out toward the car. He was angry at his mother because she wouldn't let him do what he wanted. She understood that he was angry and accepted his anger with grace. After all, from time to time, having your teen angry with you is just part of parenting.

He stormed out, tense, walking with that half-walk/half-stomp of a furious teen. He stomped to the driver's door, opened the door for his mother, stomped to the passenger door, dropped angrily into his seat, and pulled the door shut.

Mom paused for a moment pleasantly stunned that even angry, her son's gentlemanliness still extended the courtesy of opening her door for her. She knew that they would weather this little storm just fine.

LADIES AND GENTLEMEN

Before writing this chapter, I grabbed by copy of *Emily Post's Etiquette*. Flipping to the back, I note that it's 783 pages. I don't know all these rules. I don't imagine anyone knows all of them off the top of their heads. At least we have a resource if we want to look up the "rules." If in doubt, by following the rules of etiquette, we know we're following the rules of "polite society."

A core rule of being a lady or gentleman is to appreciate any legitimate effort at courtesy. For some people, it's a stretch. Some people have simply never heard of some of the rules, or they've been so often exposed to rule-breaking that they think that the custom is that thing that breaks the rule.

One that I've seen a lot and also did was to include where you're registered with an invitation. A lot of people like the convenience of having that with an invitation, but it's considered rude in polite society. Basically, any "buy me a gift" request is considered impolite. I did not know that.

I had the book, but since I've seen the registry notice in so many wedding invitations, I didn't look it up. I just assumed. That's the way it goes with most of the rules. Some we know. Some we don't know. We learn as we go.

Even when we learn some of the "rules," most polite people recognize them as guidelines. There are many casual circumstances when most of the guidelines might be excessive. That's okay.

Use the "ladies and gentlemen" guidelines when they seem appropriate. Certainly on dates and at fancier occasions, use more of them. For casual circumstances, use just some of them.

One extra guideline for ladies: never discourage any male from honoring your femininity. Some percentage of the problems women have in society are fueled in part by men failing to respect and honor women. By graciously accepting any legitimate expression of respect and courtesy, it helps encourage men to be more respectful in general.

A LIST FOR GENTLEMEN

The following is a short list of suggestions for gentlemanly behavior.

Gentlemen Make Plans with Ladies Days in Advance
Gentlemen Pick Women Up for Dates
Gentlemen Open Doors for Ladies

Gentlemen Help Women Off or On with Their Coats
Gentlemen Offer Ladies Their Coats if the Ladies are Cold
Gentlemen Give Women the Seat with the Best View
Gentlemen Pay Unless Prior Arrangements Have Been Made
Gentlemen Carry Things for Ladies
Gentlemen Walk on the Traffic Side
Gentlemen Use Polite Language in the Presence of Ladies
Gentlemen Enforce "Ladies Present" Language with Other Men
Gentlemen Respect a Woman's Words
Gentlemen Avoid Putting a Woman in a Position to Need to Stop Him
Gentlemen Avoid Raising Their Voice to a Lady
Gentlemen Honor and Cherish Women as Equals
Gentlemen Apologize When They Violate Gentlemanly Standards

A LIST FOR LADIES AND GENTLEMEN

The following is a short list of suggestions for both gentlemanly and ladylike behavior.

Ladies and Gentlemen are Generous with Compliments
Ladies and Gentlemen are Gracious when Receiving Compliments
Ladies and Gentlemen are seldom Negatively Critical, Judgmental or Condemning.
Ladies and Gentlemen are Understanding, Accepting and Discerning.
Ladies and Gentlemen Write Thank You Cards.
Ladies and Gentlemen RSVP.
Ladies and Gentlemen Apologize.
Ladies and Gentlemen Remember Names.
Ladies and Gentlemen Rescue One Another When Names are Forgotten.
Ladies and Gentlemen will Dance.
Ladies and Gentlemen are Tactful.
Ladies and Gentlemen Refrain from Unkind Remarks without Good Cause.
Ladies and Gentlemen Connect on Common Positives
Ladies and Gentlemen Minimize Even Common Negatives
Ladies and Gentlemen Keep Their Word

Ladies and Gentlemen Choose and Hold Agreed Upon Lines
Ladies and Gentlemen Say Please, Thank You and You're Welcome.

Ladies Know How to be Seated and Gentlemen Know How to Seat Ladies
Ladies Know How to Be Carried and Gentlemen Know How to Carry a Lady
Ladies Know How to Pin a Boutonnière and Gentlemen Know How to Pin a Corsage
Ladies are Understanding of Men's Appreciation of Feminine Beauty and Gentlemen are Mature and Polite About Looking

A LIST FOR LADIES

The following is a short list of suggestions for ladylike behavior.

Ladies Know How to Get In and Out of a Vehicle in a Ladylike Manner
Ladies Master the Art of the Gracious No
Ladies are Firm and Strong When Called For
Ladies Appreciate and Respect Authentic Masculinity, the Man in Men
Ladies are King Makers

SOME FINAL SUGGESTIONS

Ladies and Gentlemen continue to Learn and Grow in Etiquette
Ladies and Gentlemen understand that Etiquette is Less Common These Days
Ladies and Gentlemen Appreciate Any Legitimate Attempt at Courtesy

Remember that since etiquette is more rare today than in generations past, be gracious to those who might not know the rules. Understand that some minority of people might abuse the rules or be "etiquette police" (with stunningly self-serving interpretations in most cases). Such abuse does nothing to take away from the value of being polite.

Be a gentleman. Be a lady. In casual circumstances, employ whatever guidelines seem appropriate. For more formal occasions, use more of the guidelines. And always be encouraging of any legitimate attempt at courtesy.

CHAPTER TWENTY-SEVEN

NOBILITY: BE A LIGHT, NOT A JUDGE

It was late at night. Classes were over and the last of people had left. I was alone. I had locked up and settled down into my office to take care of a few hours of work still to be done.

Then I heard a knocking on the door. It was a familiar face: Samantha. She was the mother of students from years ago. I hadn't seen her except for the periodic social media post for years.

I unlocked the door to let her in. "I need your help," she said. "I knew I could come here and you would help me."

Just seeing our place made her feel like help was just an ask away. She explained her situation. Since I had last seen her, she got involved in an obsessive relationship with a guy, started using drugs, lost her husband, lost her children, and everything was falling apart.

She knew she needed to get off drugs. She knew that meant detox, rehab, and a lifetime of daily struggle. Every time she tried to start the process, she panicked. She knew she had to, but it terrified her to the point of panic.

For her, the answer was simple: Make smaller decisions.

What terrified her was that she was trying to change everything. If it was inspiring, that would be wonderful and I'd be all for it. Because it paralyzed her, we needed to set it aside.

"Just decide to go through detox. Then decide to go through rehab. After you're done with that, then you can decide if you want to be drug-free this week and see what it's like. If you realize that drug-free living is pretty good, you can decide to do it a while longer."

It was like the weight of the world dropped off her shoulders. "I knew you would help. I knew you wouldn't judge me or look down on me. You'd just help."

She left with Light. She had an answer. She saw. She was ready to make a smaller decision. If she thought she would find a Judge, she would not have shown up.

BE A LIGHT, NOT A JUDGE

Being a light means we provide insight and guidance.

The world is full of judgment and condemnation. Many people grow up hearing these things so often that the voice rings in their minds for the rest of their lives. Sometimes it is the voice of parents or other authorities. Sometimes it is the voice of peers. All too often, it is the self-judgment and self-condemnation learned and practiced over a lifetime.

When we say "not a judge" we mean that we do not decide that a person is bad. In this phrase, we also include "not a condemner," meaning we do not decide that a person is worthless. We distinguish between actions and identity.

When a young girl was earning "F"s in school due to missing assignments, her mother brought her to me for a talk. My talk with the girl was half for the girl's benefit and half for the mother.

After some pointed discussion done in a playful manner to reduce the sting, I asked her an important question: "Do you think I am disappointed in you?" She said no. "What am I disappointed in?" She answered correctly, "In my decisions."

143

This was important. If the girl herself and who she is were the problem, how long would it be for her to become a different person who was no longer a disappointment? Weeks? Months? Years? Ever? Depending upon how she saw it, she might think that there's no hope and she's just bad. That's not what I want for her. I want her to make better decisions.

If the girl's decisions are the problem, how quickly can she make different decisions? Immediately. Today, she can decide to do her assignments she had today. Tomorrow she can do the same. Every day she decides to actually do her work is a day to be proud of her decisions. It's an immediate fix.

I felt the girl had enough negative judgment in her life as it was. She had too many ways she was losing in life. She had too few paths to win. In the way so much of her life was going, losing was easy, winning was hard. The path to winning was too long, too hard, and seemingly out of reach.

By being a light, not a judge, she was given a way to win – and win immediately.

Sitting in judgment over others is telling them they're bad. It's telling them there's something wrong with them. It's attaching negative labels to them.

Condemning others is telling them that they're worthless. It's considering them of lower intrinsic value than you. It's treating them as unworthy of love, respect or attention.

Related to some of this is the way we bring up the past. The more we use the past as a weapon, the more we tell someone they can never, ever make things right.

Instead of being a judge, we be a light.

BE A LIGHT

To illuminate implies to bring knowledge, insight, and wisdom.

To enlighten implies teaching, edifying, and informing.

We demystify. We reduce or eliminate confusion by bringing clarity. We help someone understand. We help others see more clearly.

When Samantha came for help, she needed light. She needed to have her situation clarified for her and her problem understood. In her case, she needed to see that the decision she was grappling with was just too big. That's why it was such a struggle. Instead, she could make a smaller decision. For her, that was manageable.

I see it a lot. New college students think they are choosing the whole rest of their lives when picking a major. It's just a major. It opens certain doors and does not open other doors. It does not shackle you to a path. Just because you major in something does not mean you're going to have to do what you study for the rest of your life. It's the same with a first job out of college. It's a job, perhaps the start of a career, and if you change your mind later, that will be okay.

DEFINITION OF A PROBLEM

The definition of a problem is: something with a solution.

If something doesn't have a solution, it's not a problem. It's a fact of life. When facing a fact of life, you accept it. You adapt to it. You live with it. It's just the way it is, so we let it be and move forward anyway.

The great thing about problems is that they can be solved. If it's my problem, that means I can solve it. If it's our problem, we can solve it. If it's bigger than me or bigger than us, we get help. We may need a coach, a mentor, a teacher, or some professional to do it for us. However we get the problem solved, it's solvable.

Be a light includes helping people see the problems. Where some people might get stuck on a fact of life and keep wishing it were different, we help them see their power. We help them see answers. We help them see paths to victory. We help them see a way to win.

Then here's the hard part: We let them decide.

PEOPLE NEED MORE LIGHT-BRINGERS

Part of being a light is seeking to understand someone's situation. It's learning to see it from their point of view. It's figuring out how much they can take. Sometimes too much blunt truth is more than someone can handle right now. In the middle of their pain and confusion, they might need empathy.

As a light-bringer, we seek to bring illumination to people. We recognize that when and how we present our information is critical to communication. If we just want to have our say, we can be blunt instruments. If the goal is to help others, then we need to be a bit more artful.

As a light-bringer, part of our time might be spend just comforting someone. They're not ready for insight until they process enough of the emotion to be able to hear truth. They can be so lost in their feelings at the moment that even if they ask the questions out loud, they really aren't asking. It's rhetorical. The real answer needs to wait. Light-bringers will wait. They will empathize and comfort until someone's ready. Then they share.

There's an old saying: "They don't care how much you know until they know how much you care." Related to that, they also want to know that you really do know something. So we show our caring first. We search for the answer ourselves so we can share from a place of wisdom.

We love. We seek wisdom to share. Then we share. That's being a light. The world needs more light-bringers. The world needs more Ohana.

PART SIX
HARMONY

CHAPTER TWENTY-EIGHT

ALOHA

O-Oasis
H-Harmony
A-Assertiveness
N-Nobility
A-ALOHA

When I was six, I had my first martial art lesson. Over the years, I did Little League, some soccer, and in high school, I was a jumper in track. You'll notice there's no football.

As an adult, I was never much into sports. I might enjoy the occasional live baseball game. If a team I cared about was in an important game, I might watch. Over the years, on any given Super Bowl Sunday I would probably not be watching. I'd more likely be somewhere enjoying the lack of crowds.

I have a rule. If I love you and it's important to you, it's important to me because it's important to you. So when I had a son in football, suddenly football became important to me. I got tickets to an NFL game and took him.

Since I was going there to enjoy the game because I enjoy him, I warned him that I might have a lot of questions as we go. I understand the basics, but that's about it. I make a point to really enjoy these times because I really am there to connect with someone who matters to me.

As it worked out, he also got to witness me in action. There was a drunk who was picking fights with fans of both teams. My son said he was silently wondering if I was going to do anything about it, and I did. Quietly. Using pressure points, subtle control techniques, and de-escalation techniques. So far, he's the only current student who's actually seen first-hand what I'm like in those situations. That was an extra bonus on the specialness of the day.

I tell this story rather than a story of romantic love or commitment-through-crisis because I think it illustrates the simple every-day-ness of Aloha. Thanks to romantic movies, books, poetry and love songs, I think we have a pretty good idea of that kind of more spectacular love. Love is all those wonderful, grand, heart-stirring things. It is also the quiet, simple, every-day nature of loving connection with others.

A BASIC DEFINITION OF LOVE

"Love" is such a flexible word in English. We might use it for our child, our spouse, our sweetheart, or our parent. We could use the exact same word for a favorite pizza, drink, or a ride at Disneyland. We use the word to express devotion and commitment. We use the word to express attraction, desire, or even selfish possessiveness.

So this word would probably benefit from a definition. Here's the one we use as a basic definition of love for Ohana.

Love:
1. I want the best for you.
2. I want to be the best for you.
3. I want you to have transcendent joy.

This is such a simple, three-part definition that I've taught it to children. Six year olds get it. I also teach it to pre-teens before they hit dating age. I want them to know the difference between people who really love them and who say "love" and mean "desire."

For ourselves, it's good to evaluate how we connect with people. While we define love in terms of what we want for others, it shows up in action. In that sense, love is a verb.

MANY FACETS OF LOVE

Having a basic definition of love lets us know what we're talking about. Love is such a powerful subject that is so central to our lives that it's worthy of thought and study. So we have more!

Love shows up in all sorts of ways. To put it in general categories, we create a love stack (which is a whole lesson unto itself!).

Agape (a-GAH-pay) is unconditional love. This is character-based. It flows from who you are. If you want a very good definition of this kind of love you'll find it in the Bible at 1 Corinthians 13:4-8. Don't have a Bible handy? You can find that famous love passage at nearly any gift store. It starts "Love is patient, love is kind..."

Phileo (FIL-ee-oh) is conditional love. This is relationship-based. It flows from the interactions between the people in the relationship. The more you have positive interaction, the more positive you feel about the person. The more you have negative interactions, the more negative you feel. The important thing to know here is that negative is much more powerful than positive. It's easier to break things than it is to build things.

(I admit that while the proper pronunciation is FIL-ee-oh, I tend to pronounce it fil-AY-oh because that's how I first learned it. It also reminds the listener that I'm talking about my whole teaching on the subject.)

Eros (ee-ROS), the way I use it, is Experience or Sensation. More technically, it is the sexual component of romantic love. Using that as a model, we focus on the fact that it is the intense feelings we get with experiences that produce powerful sensations. (This is another I first learned technically incorrect and stick with my way so it's clear I'm talking about my teaching here.)

Outside the stack we have Storge (STOR-gay), or family love. This is the particular affection you tend to have for someone to whom you are related. Often, it shows up in that we give people we're related to a higher automatic starting point for relationship. We also tend to put up with more without ending the relationship.

HELLO AND GOODBYE

Aloha also means hello and goodbye. We apply it as the simple act of greeting someone when you see them and saying goodbye when you leave. Depending upon the relationship, that might include a handshake, a hug, and/or a kiss. It could include walking someone out and seeing them off.

On a deeper level, it also means "no ghosting." We used to call it dumping. It's the act of disappearing on someone without telling them its over. The simple part of aloha meaning goodbye means you don't just vanish. You break up. You say goodbye.

BE CONSISTENTLY LOVING

Love is a verb. That means it can be a habit. By practicing it consistently, we get better at it. We make it a habit so that we are consistently, habitually loving! That's the goal.

We live a life of love. People know they can count on us to be a loving person. They know that we'll be in relationship with them with the Aloha Spirit.

CHAPTER TWENTY-NINE

ALOHA: LOVE STACK: AGAPE, PHILEO, EROS

"I love you."

"No you don't."

"Yes, I do."

"No you don't."

And so it went. It got more and more intense without a single shred of useful information shared for the first several minutes of the session. Fortunately, we cut through a lot of it by discussing what love is (and what it is not) so we could turn this silly argument into a useful conversation.

"LOVE"

Love is such a generic word in English that it can mean anything. We use it for things. We love our car, our house, our new super-big television or our new phone. We love our experiences. We love that blockbuster movie, the concert, or the theme park. We love our favorite food, our favorite restaurant, walks on the beach, or a vacation destination.

Even when we're talking about people, we use the word "love" very loosely. Someone who has anxiety about being alone might claim to love a partner when all she really means is that losing her partner scares her. He might claim to love her when what he really means is that he is obsessed with her. We use love in place of attraction, in place of like, in place of lust, and in so many other ways.

love. That's why it's so important to have a working definition of love.

Our simple definition of love is in three parts.

Love.
1. I want the best for you.
2. I want to be the best for you.
3. I want you to have transcendent joy.

At least this way we know a bit more about what we're talking about. If I am looking for what I want from you rather than what I want for you, then I'm not talking about this kind of love. That's something else. It might be that I want love from you. It might be that I want something else from you. It can even be that I'd rather be in a dysfunctional relationship than all by myself. Whatever it is, we know we're not talking about this kind of love.

There's so much uncertainty around Love that few of us develop any kind of real understanding of it. Yet, at the same time, it remains one of the most powerful, most profound, most important things in our lives.

Something as important to our soul as oxygen is to our body deserves more attention than society teaches us to give it.

LOVE STACK

To understand Love beyond the three-part definition, we start with The Love Stack. The Love Stack is a simple step-pyramid. The Foundation is Character. On top of character we can then build Relationship. The capstone is Experience.

Character means we have a loving character. That makes this level of love unconditional because who I am is consistent through all my relationships. Whether you're a stranger, a friend, or my own child, I am who I am. This is Agape.

Relationship is conditional because it depends upon how we interact. The more we have positive interactions, the more positive we'll feel about each other. The more we have negative interactions, the more negatively we'll feel about each other. In time (sometimes a very short time), we come to expect either good things or bad things when we're together. We might need to put up our guard to be safe. If we know it's a good relationship, we can drop our guard, open up, and really connect. This is Phileo.

Experience is doing things together. It can be as simple as shared experiences. It can be doing things with one another that provide intense sensations. It certainly includes physical intimacy for romantic relationship. It includes anything other peak experience we have together. Something exciting for us both covers this. We use the word Eros for this in a broader, more generic sense than its Greek form.

By learning to tap into each level of The Love Stack, we can build more powerful love and more powerful, profound relationships.

Let's take a slightly closer look at each level of The Love Stack.

Note that if you ever hear me teach on this out loud, I Anglicize the pronunciation. Agape is a-GAH-pay, Phileo is fil-AY-oh, and Eros is AIR-os. Agape is essentially the same and uses a two thousand year-old definitive exploration of the word. For the others, I use a modern approach loosely based on classic Greek understanding, so please allow me to make the distinction. It provides a useful tool to explore love.

AGAPE (UNCONDITIONAL LOVE)

Unconditional Love is unique in a couple of key aspects: First, it is totally character-based. It's who you are. That's what makes it unconditional.

It also has a whole list of things it is not. This is important because "love" is often thought to include some of these things. First, love is not jealous. Jealousy is something different. Being jealous does not mean you love someone, and it does not mean someone loves you. We'll get more into this in the next chapter.

Love is not boastful or arrogant. Love is not rude or selfish. It is not prejudiced, does not hold grudges, and isn't happy over bad things happening to people. Love does not make other people responsible for your own feelings. These are things that may be taken into relationships along with love, but those things are not love. They can be separated, and we would do well to separate them. Those things tend to do harm to relationships.

The positive character traits that are love include patience, kindness, and forgiveness. It includes putting up with things, going through things alongside one another, and holding to hope through the dark times. It includes look for truth and rejoicing in its discovery. Unconditional love lasts because it is who you are.

The study of unconditional love is a worthy investment of time. As of this writing, I have a 24-lesson program I've produced on the subject. It could easily be a book. Certainly it is worthy of a study far deeper than the chapter-and-a-half treatment I can give it in this book!

PHILEO (CONDITIONAL LOVE)

A common teaching is that unconditional love is good and conditional love is bad. That's not actually true – not by the definitions we use here. Conditional love means the love changes based upon the relationship. To say that Phileo is inferior to Agape is to say that relationships are inferior to character. They are just different things.

Relationship is built on character. If you and I are in a relationship, who I am as a person comes to the relationship. Who you are as a person comes to the relationship. We build our relationship starting with who I am and who you are, and then we enjoy experiences together. That's how we build a relationship.

Phileo Love works on a principle I call The Phileo Bank Account. A few others have taught similar principles, including Stephen Covey, John Maxwell, and Willard Harley. Something overlooked in other models is a simple and important truth: Negative is more powerful than positive.

In short, it's easier to break things than it is to build things. The ratio seems to about four to one. Think of it this way. Most of life is pretty neutral. Those are zero-point items that neither build up nor tear down relationships. They're just sort of there. It's the normal day-to-day routines we do to accomplish the business of life.

Then there are positive events and negative events. Those are worth points. Suppose an event is worth 1 to 4 points. If it's a positive event, you get 1 to 4 points. If you keep having neutral and positive interactions, you'll keep gaining points.

Negative interactions, though, are another matter. Sure, they're worth 1 to 4 points, too, but… negative is four times more powerful than positive! A 1-point negative event multiplies by 4 for a loss of 4 points. A 4-point disaster (like a horrible fight with terrible things said and done that should never said and should never be done) costs 16 points, not just 4.

Then, of course, there are negative things that rise to the level of "deal breaker." Those are things bad enough that if they happen, it's over, period. Deal breakers don't have a positive counterpart. There aren't any things that are so good that if they happen it guarantees a great relationship forever.

Building relational love is an ongoing adventure. We constantly and consistently add to a relationship with positive experiences.

EROS (EXPERIENCE LOVE)

Experiences are powerful. When we remember life, we remember moments. When we think of our childhood, we think of a collection of individual memories. We don't have an 18-year video that runs in our head. We have specific moments we remember. There may be a lot of them, but they are still a collection of moments.

Emotional meaning makes events memorable. Uniqueness and intensity make events memorable. Building Eros on purpose is intentionally seeking High Points. We craft experiences to make them more meaningful. We enjoy things together that mean something to both of us. We seek the kind of experiences that give both us the kind of sensations we find exciting.

LOVE STACK

The simple application of The Love Stack is to begin with who we are as individuals. We can continue to learn, grow and mature on our own or in relationship with others. Then we build our individual relationships. In those relationships, we seek to build memorable moments through experience and sensation.

This gives is a model to think about love. It gives us a way to define it for clearer communication. It helps us diagnose what areas we might want to enhance and lets us have useful discussions. That's part of the purpose and power of having clean definitions: effective communication.

CHAPTER THIRTY

ALOHA: LOVE IS NOT JEALOUS AND DOES NOT ENVY

She was a flirt. He knew that when they started dating.

So when they started dating and she kept flirting with other guys, he wasn't surprised. He had already accepted it as part of having a relationship with a woman who enjoyed her flirtations. She never took it beyond playful flirting, so he left it alone.

Until one day she complained about his acceptance of her flirting. "If you loved me," she said, "you'd be jealous!"

THERE ARE THINGS LOVE IS NOT

Often in our culture some things show up so often in love-relationships that we just assume they are part of love. Some people say that unless someone is jealous or territorial, they don't love you. Some claim that the only reason they lose their temper is because they love someone. Some people attach all sorts of unhealthy behavior to "love."

However, these things are not love. They are something else. This idea that these common things are part of love is not new. The importance of making sure we understand that these things are not love is also not new.

It was two thousand years ago that this list of what love is not had to be taught. If we're being told this list of things that love is not, it's a pretty safe bet that love has been misunderstood for all of human history.

Thus, no matter how common it might be to mix these negative things into what we think of as love, it's important to for us to know better. We should know that when these things show up, it's not love. Any of them might be there along with love, but these things are not love.

LOVE IS NOT...

Love is Not Jealous. Jealousy is born out of insecurity. It's important to understand that jealousy is not the same as love. It does not tell you that you love someone. It also does not tell you that someone loves you. Sometimes there is reason to feel insecure because the relationship actually does lack security. Most of the time it's just a feeling. An empowered response to feeling jealous is to step up your own game.

Love Does Not Envy. Envy is taking good news for someone else as bad news for you. Sometimes people don't like other people getting stuff – including compliments or attention – unless they're getting even more. Love is treating good news for others as good news! Enjoy good things coming to those whom you love!

Love Does Not Boast. It's bragging if it isn't true, and even if it is true, it's bragging when it's stealing someone's spotlight. Of course, never lie about yourself. Even when a truth about you might out-shine someone, when it's someone's turn to be the star, let them be the star. When someone else is the center of attention, let them be the center of attention.

Love is Not Rude. Some people think that being in a love-relationship means they can be mean. Being in a love-relationship some people take as permission to be at their worst. While being comfortable with one another is good, The Upgrade Principle says they deserve more of your best.

Love Does Not Act Unbecomingly. Love does not embarrass others. The simple thing here is to behave appropriate to the circumstances for the sake of others if not yourself.

Love is Not Selfish. Love focuses on others. Sometimes, the desire to be loved can be selfish. The desire to love is not selfish. Remember the fundamentals of love are that I want the best for you and to be the best for you.

Love is Not Prejudiced. Love does not pre-judge. Some things you might hold loosely based upon what is statistically true, but everyone is an individual.

Love is Not Provoked. Being in a love relationship might put you in proximity to be provoked, but it's not the love itself that gets you provoked. Love isn't why anyone gets angry. Love is always a positive emotion.

Love Does Not Make Others Responsible for Its Emotions. This is larger than just provocation to anger. In general, if I have a loving character, I do not make anyone else responsible for my emotions, good or bad. Others can only be responsible for their behavior, not my feelings. Love recognizes that my feelings are my responsibility.

Love Does Not Hold Grudges. Love forgives. We all know we should. Forgiveness is a skill that only a few of us have been taught. I teach a powerful forgiveness system you'll find in two of my books and in my programs. As I point out, anyone who does not want to forgive has been taught incorrect information on what forgiveness is and what it is not. Unfortunately, there's only a little really good teaching on forgiveness and how to do it.

Love Does Not Count Events as Patterns. None of us are perfect. We'll all make mistakes. We'll all mess up in our own ways, sometimes in small ones, and sometimes in big ones. There is a difference between a pattern and an event. If someone has a positive pattern and a negative event happens, love recognizes that the event is the exception and not the rule. We look at who people are by the patterns of their behavior.

Love Does Not Like Bad Things Happening to People. Sometimes we get angry with people. Sometimes people hurt us or our loved ones so badly we want nothing to do with them. In and of themselves, both of those are okay. When people get appropriate consequences for bad behavior, that's a good thing. When people suffer, even people we do not like, love never enjoys it.

Love Does Not Like People Doing Bad Things. Sometimes people do bad things that benefit us. Some people think some bad things are cool. Most of us remember that "cool kids" in school were often rule-breakers. Love never sees people doing bad things as a good thing.

OHANA SEEKS WHAT LOVE IS

By realizing that all these things are not part of love, we all learn that these are things to be avoided rather than sought. Far too often we accept these "not love" things as love. If we recognize that they are not love, then we know that when they show up alongside love, that a maturing love should get rid of them.

Ohana seeks what love is. Ohana seeks to avoid what love is not. Certainly as Ohana, we do not interpret what love is not as love!

CHAPTER THIRTY-ONE

ALOHA: PHILEO BANK ACCOUNT: POSITIVE ON PURPOSE

Suddenly he leapt to his feet and sprinted for the door.

I couldn't see what suddenly had him so excited, but whatever it was it prompted him to run to the door and go outside.

He spotted Nancy. He and Nancy always had fun together. Seeing her show up had gotten more and more exciting over the years. Now it was worth jumping to his feet and sprinting to meet her before she even got to the door!

PHILEO

We use Phileo Love as the conditional love of relationships. It's how we distinguish one person from another. Since Agape Love is driven by character, it's unconditional. That means it's the same for everyone.

Of course we have friends, we have loved ones, we have people whose company we seek out more than others. If all any relationship took was the kind of unconditional love that is driven by our good character, we could randomly select anyone in the world for any kind of relationship. Obviously, that's not what we do. We favor some individuals over others. We favor our own personally special people over random strangers.

That's Phileo. It's conditional love that we build through the quality of our relationship. The more we have positive interactions, the more we get along, the stronger our love-relationship. At its simplest, we just keep doing good things and we build the relationship.

Sometimes people get comfortable in relationships and go to their own default behaviors. Most of our behavior is relatively neutral. Some of it is positive, and some of it is negative. When people have longstanding relationships, sometimes it's easy to give themselves permission to be at their worst. Rather, we should give more of our best.

We should seek to be positive on purpose. We'll do enough negative things by mistake and when we're upset to do some damage to a relationship. Therefore, it's important to understand how to keep a relationship growing and to understand what happens to our relationships when we behave badly.

PHILEO BANK ACCOUNT

The Phileo Bank Account is a way to think about how the conditional love of relationship works.

Stephen Covey's version is called the Emotional Bank Account. John Maxwell talks about "change," that you can effect change if your previous positive interactions have built up relationship currency you can spend to get change to happen. Willard Harley teaches a version he calls the Love Bank.

Each of these models has value. Something overlooked in each one, though, is the bad things do more damage than we think. At their worst, a bad thing can be a deal breaker. Something really, really bad happening just a few times, or even just once, can be enough to end a friendship or a romance.

There is no positive counterpart to a deal breaker. That would be something that could be done just one time or just a few times that would forever keep a relationship positive. There's so such great and grand gesture a person can do that will make love everlasting no matter how someone behaves in the future.

In short, it's easier to break things than it is to build things. If we understand this, we have a powerful insight that helps us build and protect every relationship we have: romances, friendship, and business relationships.

NEGATIVE IS FOUR TIMES MORE POWERFUL THAN POSITIVE

Gary Smalley is one of the relationship experts that takes note of how negative things affect us. He uses the metaphor of a stone. When we do negative things, we see them as small pebbles we're dropping on the relationship. Then our ridiculous partner totally over-reacts to a silly little pebble. What Smalley notes, though, is that when it hits the other person, it's not a tiny little pebble. When it hits the other person, it's a great big rock.

We often don't realize that bad things have a multiplied effect. The approximate ratio is four to one. It takes four points of building to balance one point of breaking.

If we think about events as worth 1 to 4 points, it helps. Positive events gain between 1 and 4 points. A negative event would also be worth 1 to 4 points, but because negative is four times more powerful than positive, we multiply negative events by four. The makes a negative event worth 4 to 16 points on the debit column of the Phileo Bank Account.

The situation is a little bit worse than that, though. When we do negative things, they are almost always worse than we think. So we add a point to the negative thing before we multiply. That makes our range of 1 to 4 into a range of 2 to 5, and then we multiply by four for a loss of 8 to 20 points when we do something negative.

The formula is this: P=n (positive equals the number).
N=(n+1)4 (negative equals the number plus one quantity times four).

Does it work precisely like this? Of course not. This only approximates what happens to the relationship-love with positive and negative interaction. It reminds us to be positive on purpose and to never give ourselves permission to be our worst in our relationships.

The Phileo Bank Account model allows us to dive into a lot of powerful concepts that include chunking, de-chunking, how forgiveness affects it, and so many other interesting insights. Get my program on Relationship Love to really learn all the powerful things you can do with this model. It really is amazing.

NEGATIVE HUMOR

The Phileo Bank Account also tells us what happens with negative humor. If someone makes a funny joke at your expense, they get a point for funny and lose a point for negative.

The multiplier still takes effect, though! We get one point for funny and the negative point multiplies by four, so we have a net loss of three points. If we make too many jokes at someone's expense, even if they really, honestly thought every single joke was funny, we're damaging and may lose the relationship.

If the person doesn't think it's funny at all, then we lose even more points faster. The idea of "forget them if they can't take a joke" will lead to a lot of ended relationships.

POSITIVE ON PURPOSE

The Phileo Bank Account reminds us to be Positive On Purpose. Maintain the intention to build every relationship we have by being positive. We can be the friend that our friends look forward to seeing. We can be the family member that our family is happy is coming over for the holidays.

Even in our casual, momentary relationship, by being positive, we can add to other's days. By being the pleasant customer, we can add to the day of a clerk. The relationships can be that casual and that fleeting, and the idea of being positive on purpose can make a powerful difference.

That's Ohana.

CHAPTER THIRTY-TWO

ALOHA: LOVE, JOY, PEACE

It was the middle of a mess. Bankruptcy loomed as a very real threat. The 2008 economic crisis was tearing into households all across the country. I watched as Alexander and Susan were losing it all.

Yet somehow in the middle of it all, they still gazed into one another's eyes with love. In the middle of it all, they still found a thousand simple joys in which to take pleasure. While chaos swirled all around them, they found their moments of peace.

To be perfectly frank, a great deal of their resilience was born out of their faith in God. They had a much bigger picture in mind than the disaster they were facing.

Life was bigger than this moment. They said that what they were going through was terrible. There was no denying that. But it wasn't the whole story, and it wasn't the end of the story.

They had a large view of their lives. Love, joy, and peace were anchored in those larger truths. It gave them strength to hold to these spiritual things in the middle of worldly chaos.

LOVE

Love is the highest value in creation. The Bible tells us that God so loved the world that He gave His Son, which is the fundamental foundation for all of Christianity. The whole religion of Christianity exists because of love. The Bible even goes so far as to say that God IS love.

We've already talked about many aspects of it. From the basic three-point definition to diving in to The Love Stack, what love is not, and how relationship-love works. I have dozens of hours and uncounted pages written on the subject. We've already spent so much time on it, let's assume we understand it deeply enough to elevate how well we life a life of love.

JOY

When we talk about love, the third part of our three-part definition is "I want you to have transcendent joy!" This joy is like a deeply persistent happiness. It's so big, so well established, and so powerful that it endures chaos. It shines through difficult times. It brings a smile to your face even in the midst of disaster.

Let's build up our understanding from pleasure to happiness to joy. Pleasure is momentary. You experience pleasure while it is happening, and once it's over, it's over. When you're eating a favorite sweet, you have the pleasure of the taste until you're done eating. Once the taste fades, so does the pleasure.

Happiness is something a bit bigger than pleasure. A simple way to be happy is to remember pleasures. Happiness means you have some particular rules you've learned or that experience has given you, and those rules are being followed. Some people have really, really difficult happiness rules. Things must be "just so" for them, which means they are rarely (if ever) happy. Others have really simple, easy happiness rules, so they spend most of their time happy.

The fastest, most persistent path to happiness is gratitude. Happy means you're thinking pleasant thoughts most of the time. The fastest way to get there and stay there is to practice an attitude of gratitude. The definition of Attitude of Gratitude is "be thankful for everything you would not want to lose." That definition reminds us to take a look at the good things we might take for granted. The more we look at things we like, the happier we'll feel.

Joy is even bigger than happiness. Joy persists through difficult times because it is anchored to larger truths. Think of it this way. When we have a "really good" workout, we usually mean we're sweaty, sore, and exhausted. Sometimes we're even in pain. But we consider it a "really good" workout. Why? Because we understand that it is connected with a larger truth. In this case, the big win is the body we're developing. Joy is like that.

Joy means we understand that the universe works on rules, and that those rules are designed for us to be able to win. Religious people often see that winning doesn't even have to happen here and now. The win can be in eternity. Christians see heaven as an ultimately large truth and their certainty that it awaits is an ultimate win. It helps a great many people endure all sorts of terrible things. Even the loss of loved ones is tempered by a certainty of seeing then again.

Joy can be based on rules that apply in this life, too. Napoleon Hill from *Think And Grow Rich* fame taught that every bad thing has in it the seed of an equal or greater benefit. By his teaching, no matter how bad things get, there is a way for it to serve a role in things working out for good in the long run. This is also an ancient idea. The Bible says that all things work together for good, too, subject to certain conditions.

The feeling that this is not the end of the story helps us be joyful in hard times. The modern proverb of "when you're going through hell, keep going" reminds us that the worst parts are not the end.

Even if we think of a "fairy tale life," we are reminded that between "once upon a time" and "they lived happily ever after" the story gets pretty bleak. Yet the story still ends with "happily ever after." These ideas can give people joy, that special kind of happiness that depends upon one's belief in a big-picture win. Joy can even stand in defiance of what this moment may be like. That's the power of Joy.

PEACE

Peace has many forms.

One is to actually help create and preserve peace – as in lack of conflict and lack of violence. That's the goal of the Guardian Arts. Our goal is to protect the peace, and if peace is broken, our goal is to restore it. If violence is made necessary by another's violent choices, the goal is to stop evil and restore the peace as effectively and efficiently as possible.

This philosophy extends from the obvious violence of physical conflict to the less obvious: conflict in relationships. We do not wish to add unnecessarily to physical conflict nor initiate it. Likewise, we do not wish to add to relationship conflict nor initiate that conflict. Sometimes it may be necessary (as parents can attest).

The short version of this is that we don't pick fights. When someone starts to pick a fight with us, we don't participate in the stair-step escalation. If someone wants to create a fight, they'll have to do it all by themselves. We'll keep things calm and talk, or if we can't keep them calm, we'll excuse ourselves.

That's one way we protect the peace in our Ohana.

Another form of peace is to have inner peace. It's easy to have inner peace when things are peaceful. In fact, during peaceful times, we benefit greatly from relaxing and really taking in the moment. For many people, being out in nature is peaceful. Pausing to really experience that peace is powerful.

In the middle of chaos, we can remember that peaceful feeling. We can go back to those peaceful moments in our mind to relax in trying times. That's one way to do it.

Another is much like joy. We focus on larger truths. We focus on the big picture and find peace in the moment because it's part of a bigger picture. We put the moment in perspective by looking at it from a higher perspective. This can be difficult for most people. It is a skill well worth developing.

MORE SPIRITUALITY

The list of spiritual virtues continues. It includes patience and kindness, the foundation stones of agape love. Goodness, a particular kind of goodness, is also a part of being our higher and better self. This sort of goodness is being good in nature and beneficial in effect.

Faith is part of it. So is gentleness, that special kind of gentle that is really only possible for the strong. When you have great strength or great power, and you have such excellent control that you can be gentle with others, that's a virtue. Self-control is the capstone.

All of these are well worth exploring more deeply as part of being Ohana.

CHAPTER THIRTY-THREE

ALOHA: GOD, PEOPLE, SELF

"Thank you for disobeying the Bible in this," I said.

Why in the world would I be thanking a Christian woman for disobeying the Bible? Because there is a verse in the Bible that says to love your neighbor as yourself.

I had seen how she loved herself. I'd seen how she endless peppered herself with judgment and condemnation. I saw how she chastised herself, insulted herself, believed the worst of her worth, and believed herself unworthy of love.

Certainly I would not have wanted anyone speaking to me saying the kind of things she so often said to herself. I would not have wanted that from her. If someone spoke to me in such a manner as often as she did to herself, I would not have considered it very loving.

"Perhaps," I suggested, "you might want to consider loving yourself the same way you love others."

LOVE GOD

In Christianity, the highest love is to love God. In both Matthew and Mark loving God is the greatest commandment. The Mark version has the greatest amplification: Love the Lord your God with all of your heart, with all of your soul, and with all of your mind."

Then there's an interesting statement in 1 John 4. "He who does not love his brethren whom he has seen, how can he love God whom he has not seen?" The idea here seems to be that if you intend to love God, you practice with people.

So part of loving God is to love people.

LOVE PEOPLE

The greatest commandment is to love God. Without being asked, Jesus added this: "The second is like the first, you shall love your neighbor as yourself."

Loving God would be the highest Christian value. John tells us that to really love God, we should also be loving people. We are told to love our neighbors. We are told to love the brethren.

Curiously, and perhaps most difficult of all, we are also told to love our enemies. This can be a particularly difficult test of our love. While agape is unconditional, it is certainly not unlimited. Our enemies will test our patience and ability to be kind. It can be difficult to have a positive phileo-relationship with someone determined to be nasty. Yet we do our best anyway, whatever our best may be. Often our best may be simply to stay away.

There is an interesting piece in both Mark and Matthew. That of loving your neighbor as yourself. There is an implication there that we should have a healthy sort of love for ourselves, and love others in like manner.

LOVE YOURSELF

If we love others the way we love ourselves, then we should love ourselves in the same way we know we should love others. Our love for others should be healthy and helpful. Our love for ourselves should also be helpful and healthy.

Think of the chain. We have a good and healthy love for ourselves. Then we love others as we love ourselves. As we love others whom we have seen, we then love God whom we have not seen. It's all connected.

The importance of a healthy love-of-self (as opposed to an unhealthy self-indulgence) is also reflected in the idea that we are God's temple and that God's spirit dwells in us.

An interesting insight in relationships includes that I take care of you and you take of me. An even deeper, thoughtful insight is that I take care of me for you, and you take care of you for me. We take care of ourselves and extend that self-care like love to others, too.

The key is to have a healthy love all around: self, others, God. The love being healthy is the key. This is Ohana, and remembering that as we are Ohana for others, we also do it all for ourselves.

PART SEVEN
MAKING IT HAPPEN

CHAPTER THIRTY-FOUR

INTRODUCING OHANA INTO YOUR ORGANIZATION

My Ohana stories slide between those I've been Ohana for, those who have been Ohana for me, and stories of clients. Ohana behavior is so common in my life that people are sometimes shocked when it doesn't happen.

Even so, we're not perfect. As you try to do Ohana, you'll find that you're not perfect at it – no matter how long you practice. Neither is anyone else. You'll get better. So will they – if they're working at it.

There's a lot here. As quickly as we've covered Oasis, Harmony, Assertiveness, Nobility, and Aloha here, it's still a lot. The dive into the five-by-five makes for a total of thirty chapters to study. Even then, the study just scratches the surface.

You can go far, far deeper if you like.

On the flip side, you can also start light. If you want to introduce the idea of Ohana to your group or organization, begin with *The Ohana Way Report*. That book is this book, except much shorter. It lacks the twenty-five chapters of the five-by-five. It makes for much faster reading. It's less of a stretch for most people's thinking.

STARTING LIGHT: THE OHANA WAY REPORT

In *The Ohana Way Report*, we just touch on the surface level of OHANA. We talk about Oasis, Harmony, Assertiveness, Nobility, and Aloha. As noted at the end of each chapter, there are five areas for a deeper dive under each of them. That's The Ohana Five-by-Five.

We've made the deeper dive in *The Ohana Way*, so you've got Ohana coming in loud and clear. The signal is strong. (The five-by-five metaphor is originally from radio broadcasts, if you didn't already know and have forgotten from earlier in the book.)

Defining Ohana clearly (defining anything clearly, for that matter) helps us have conversations when something isn't quite right. It provides for starting points when you're building something new. It provides individual elements as you go.

The power of *The Ohana Way Book* is that it provides the 25 important concepts that enhance and enrich the core five ideals of Ohana. By exploring the subject in more depth, you can find places that may need more attention. You can choose to focus on one thing at a time.

For instance, if you were to bring *The Ohana Way* into a business environment, you might start with the basics of "family" and "no one gets left behind" and "no one gets forgotten" for the first few weeks. Breaking inertia can take effort. You may already find that you have some tough conversations needed. If you're the leader, it's best to have already read the whole book and gotten into 4P360 and YORI a bit. That way you're ready if team members bring up difficult things.

While it's in my best interests to sell you more books and programs, I would start with *The Ohana Way Report*.

First, it's inexpensive. Before you invest too much getting too deep, start with the report. It's a very solid start, and the report is short enough that it's not at all intimidating. No one will hold a copy of the report in their hands and wonder when the heck they'll ever have time to read something so thick. It's short. It's quick. It's inexpensive.

Second, you can get a very good sense of whether you have resistance to the idea. Depending upon the nature of your team's culture, Ohana might be an easy fit... or not so easy a fit. Depending upon what you do and how you do it, you might find that your people just aren't interested.

My experience shows that a lack of interest in this usually means that they don't trust it. If the team doesn't trust the leadership because of the "program of the month" syndrome or "buzzword of the year" syndrome, then, to them, it's just one more program for the sake of a program, and they don't expect anything from it. If that's the case, the solution is simple: Leaders Go First.

The other form of not trusting it is if team members think that leadership is doing this as some sort of manipulation. If leaders either have a demonstrated history of not respecting team members as whole people, the distrust might be warranted. It might take some time to earn that trust. In this case, the solution is also simple: Leaders Go First. (You notice there's a theme here.)

If there is a need for leaders to go first, then the team members can have the report for their own edification while the leadership goes through *The Ohana Way Book* or *The Ohana Way Program*. *The Ohana Way Report* will give the team enough to know what's going on so they can watch the leaders and see for themselves.

There's a very good chance that *The Ohana Way* will be very appealing to any team of people. Whether you're in a small group or a large organization, the ideals of Ohana are attractive – for those who believe it can be real. Certainly I've seen it be real!

In that case, *The Ohana Way Book* and *The Ohana Way Program* together are powerful. Or one or the other. Or have me in for live training. Or combine them in any way that serves your organization.

You've read *The Ohana Way*. Just imagine if you had more Ohana in your life. Imagine getting up in the morning with your home-Ohana, heading off to spend the day working with your work-Ohana, heading to your martial arts school to train with your dojo-Ohana, and then back home to your home-Ohana.

What a life that would be! And you can be a part of making that true by starting with this simple admonition: Be Ohana!

CHAPTER THIRTY-FIVE

IMPLEMENTING OHANA BY STEALTH

I had just finished teaching a seminar on Ohana and a man rushed up to ask me a question. "How can I implement this at work?"

He went on to explain that his workplace was a toxic environment. They did not invest in training. They certainly would not invest in something as "fuzzy" as "culture development." If he tried to implement any of this stuff, he'd be laughed out of the company!

Of course, I assume he's using a bit of hyperbole, but I get the problem. Often you're not in the right leadership position to make a decision about implementing something like Ohana. Even if you are, sometimes your company culture is so opposed to intentional growth that it would be rejected immediately.

What do you do?

The answer is relatively simple: Start with Invisible Steps.

THE INVISIBLE STEP

A young lady really needed to know she was loved, but she could not hear the words. She would not believe the words. Who could love her? Why would this family love her? If you said, "I love you" to her, she'd freak out a little. What did you mean by that? What did you really want? What were you up to?

179

Instead, the family used the three-part definition of love: I want the best for you, I want to be the best for you, and I want you to have transcendent joy. The first level was for the young lady to recognize that the family wanted the best for her. That took a few weeks, but she started to understand that much, at least. When asked, she could say that she definitely saw that in them.

They had already been working to be the best for her. Given who they were and who she was and what she needed, they sought to be what she needed from them. As it turned out, her needs would dramatically escalate when her family was suddenly homeless. There wasn't room in the shelter for them all, so one of the daughters needed a place to stay. The family took her in.

She saw that they really were exactly the kind of people she needed, and they were ready to step up. Then she saw how much they wanted her joy. She was included with the family. Later on when the rest of her family could no longer stay at the shelter, they all stayed with the family until they got new housing.

It took months, but finally she recognized the truth. The family wanted the best for her. The family wanted to be the best for her. They wanted her to have a shot at happiness and to know how to get there, which is a huge part of joy. As she had learned this is what love is, she saw that they loved her. Then she could hear the words. Then she could say the words.

The family had taken a lot of invisible steps to "I love you." Rather than impose the words on a young lady who could not hear them, they had a clean definition, they did what love is, and they taught her what it was.

A decade later she is still very comfortable with the words "I love you." She says them freely. She still has a good relationship with all of the members from that family.

START WITH THE DEFINITION

Rather than say what you're doing with the label, describe what you're doing with the principle.

Let's take Assertiveness. It's moving forward on purpose with respect for others. Rather than label it assertiveness, just start with whatever piece might need to be underscored. Maybe it's deciding on "forward," or deciding on "purpose" or doing it "more respectfully."

Even a generally negative culture will typically recognize that if you define a target, you're more likely to hit it. That helps set up "forward." If you know what you hope to accomplish with your "forward," that's "purpose," the bigger the picture the better. "Respect for others" is a great way to keep the best people on your team and the best way to keep customers coming back. Even a toxic culture might see a selfish utility in that.

Without ever mentioning the word Assertive, without ever mentioning the word Ohana, and without anyone even knowing you're using this book, you've just introduced the concept of Assertiveness into the company culture. You've taken a small, invisible step that makes things better.

You can do this with the five primary concept or with any of the twenty-five of the Ohana Five-by-Five. You can use a similar technique in any group. Friends, family, and even children can easily learn the principles of Ohana and the Ohana Five-by-Five.

REPEAT, REPEAT, REPEAT

If you can keep the number of concepts you try to introduce down to just one, it's easier to keep the steps invisible. One at a time is easier to implement. Even if you're going to do more, keep it to no more than three new concepts at a time.

When you feel one has been adopted, you can move on to another while continuing the practice of the one you helped introduce.

Even if a group decides together they want to become Ohana, you will still use a similar process. Just focus on one to three at a time until the group is doing it well. Then add another. It's also the way you teach it to children - just one to three at a time.

YOU GO FIRST

A powerful way to keep things moving is to be a great example of it.

There's a better than 7 in 10 chance that if someone quits a job, they are leaving the people, not the work. Most people who quit jobs go look for other work in the same field. Whether they find it or not, just the fact that most people quit and look for similar work shows it's not the work they leave. Part of your job is to be one of the people others want to work with.

In family relationships, part of your job is to make sure you're easy to get along with. You might also run interference with known problem family members. Follow the Ohana principles yourself and slowly introduce them to your family the same way you might do it by stealth in a work environment. Or get a copy of the book for family members that might be good allies!

Ohana is powerful. In your personal relationships, If your friends and romantic partners see you as an Oasis, even just that alone is enough to sustain almost all relationships. Knowing how to be together while being different, leaving out the parts that damage this particular relationship, can sustain almost all relationships up to friendships. Even in more intimate relationships, if you can cooperate on being partners rather than opponents, you'll have those relationships a long time, too.

If when you try to get things done, you have a definite forward, you have purpose, and you show respect, that alone can sustain relationships. If you live up to your highest and best self, that makes a huge difference everywhere. If you also learn to treat people like they matter and you want the best for them, you've got the whole Ohana package going for you.

You can easily see how great it would be to have Ohana-behavior in your intimate relationships, your families, your workplaces, and your friendships. It IS great! So we go first.

ALWAYS BE READY TO GIVE AN ANSWER

If you introduce the principles of Ohana or Ohana Five-by-Five a little at a time, eventually someone is likely to ask about what you're doing. If you get past the half-way mark without anyone asking, be prepared to share even if not asked. This presupposes that there is a clear enough improvement that you're confident they would like the rest!

Be ready to explain the principles of Ohana or the whole Ohana Five-by-Five. Or you could just give them a copy of the book, either *The Ohana Way Report* or the full book, *The Ohana Way.* Or, if you have it, the audio program *The Ohana Way Program.*

Even if you give someone the book, be prepared to sit down and have a discussion about it. If you've been introducing concepts into the group, chances are you'll be seen as the expert. An easy way to lead a group on the topic is to do a book study. I advise you first cover the five basic principles of Ohana. Then go back through them a second time and dive into the Five-by-Five.

If you focus on just one principle a week, you'll invest more than half-a-year in the process. That's slowly enough that a group that does okay should be able to improve in most of them. If everyone has a copy of the book and can read ahead, you may see better results.

CHAPTER THIRTY-SIX

IMPLEMENTING OHANA WITH A COOPERATIVE TEAM

A cooperative team is a magnificent treasure. Even if you started with "leaders go first" or you introduced Ohana by stealth, in time, nearly any team may be ready to do it on purpose.

Most people who have tried to institute behavioral change in any kind of existing group report that it's difficult to do. Failure often comes simply because we lack a technique to do it.

Here's a simple one that works exceptionally well.

OHANA QUANTIFIER

First, assign a number to where you are. For starters, just do it with the fundamentals of The Five as a group: Oasis, Harmony, Assertiveness, Nobility, and Aloha. Later you can focus on just one aspect or on any one of the Five-by-Five.

Rate from -10 to +10.

Negative numbers mean you feel your team does a really bad job of it. It's possible. Some cultures have gotten so toxic that they literally chase people away. Some companies have lost their best team members due to culture. If the number is negative, it's negative. That's okay. You want to know what you have to start with.

Neutral numbers mean that the group is neither a plus or minus culturally. It just sort of "is." Sometimes I've asked people about their work culture, and they say things like, "I don't know... it's just work. I guess we don't think about it." If you put a number on that, it might range from about -1 to maybe a 2 or 3. Middling positive numbers are pretty good. Higher positive numbers are very good. And when you get to the 8 to 10 range, that's exceptional.

Everyone participating on the team gives their number.

It's best if this is done confidentially. You'll get better answers if there's no way to know what number any given person gave. Ideally, do not have a team member tally the scores. Definitely do not have a leader tally the score.

Where Are We?

Where are we? Commonly groups that work well together and have a pretty decent company culture will average around a 5 or 6. Total up the numbers, divide them by the number of people participating, and you'll get your starting number. It is what it is.

Why would the numbers be between a 5 and 6? Some leaders get very concerned with this number. Remember, we're looking at an area to improve. So of course the number should leave room for improvement. The number should not be 8 or higher already or there isn't much room to get better!

What about lower numbers? This is not necessarily bad news. It is an honest assessment of where you are. It means there's plenty you can do. Almost any element of Ohana, even the easiest to implement, will bump that up. If you have a zero-ish number or a negative number, you should use that to motivate implementation!

Where Do We Want To Be?

Where do we want to be? The "obvious" answer is, "Ten! Of course!" Actually, not necessarily.

Much more commonly, people think a good target is between an 8 and 9. We get sayings in sales and motivation like "anything less than a 10 is just a 4 in disguise," but puffed up 10s often deflate quickly.

185

A number that feels both real and achievable usually works best. Most people report that "10" feels more like hype and emotion than a real target. Expect it may just be an 8 or 9. Any number is okay, even a 10, or a 5 (especially if you're starting in negative territory). Just let the number be the number.

Typically, there is about a three-point difference between where you are and where the group thinks they ought to be and can achieve.

WHAT TO START WITH

Ohana includes Oasis, Harmony, Assertiveness, Nobility, and Aloha. The Five-by-Five includes five more lessons under each for a total of thirty possibilities. If you include Ohana as a general principle, that makes thirty-one. Where do you start?

You'll actually work on two things at the same time: A group thing and a personal thing. Everyone in the group will work on the same one thing. Then everyone in the group will pick one thing of their own to work on.

The Group Thing

First, choose the thing the group will work on. The group decides.

Here's the question: "What can we focus on as a group that we can do successfully that will help us get one or two points towards our goal?"

Then let them vote. You may choose another secret vote or just do this by a show of hands. It's a judgment call. If you're not sure, make it another secret vote. Remember: The leader does NOT tally the votes. Whichever gets the most votes is what the group will work on. If there's a tie, just ask for a show of hands between those two. At that level there is typically not much need for another secret vote.

Any of the five, thirty, or thirty-one is a good place to start. You really can't go wrong with this.

The Personal Thing

Then each team member will pick one thing to work on individually. Again, there is no wrong answer. Any one of the pieces of Ohana or the Ohana Five-by-Five will make a positive difference.

Each individual uses nearly the same question: "What can I focus on as an individual that I can succeed at that will help me contribute to our goal?"

Here I suggest Whole Person thinking. I think it's a good idea to pick something that will help in the Whole Person's Whole Life. If working on a particular trait will make a difference at work, at home, and with friends, that will be exceptionally useful! Pick one of those.

FEED FORWARD

We know where we are. We know where we want to go. We know what we're working on as a group. Each of us knows what we're working on as an individual. That's a great start!

Now what? Now we get some ideas.

The technique is called "Feed Forward." A great thing about Feed Forward is that you don't need to know anything about the person or group to do it. Here's all you do: Ask a quick question, get a quick answer, thank them, move on.

Let's suppose the group decided to work on "Oasis." My individual thing is "I Have a Point; You May Also Have a Point" from Assertiveness. This would be my question:

"I'm working on Oasis and I Have a Point; You May Also Have a Point. Could you give me one or two quick ideas I might be able to do to improve on those?"

Then I listen.

Here's the trick that really makes this work. I don't judge the idea. I don't argue with it. I don't say I already do that. I don't say that someone else already said that. I don't say it's a good idea. I don't say anything about the idea.

I just say, "Thank you." Then I write a quick note for me to remember the suggestions.

Why don't I grade the idea? Because everyone should be free to just give their ideas. Maybe that idea that you might think is stupid for you might be exactly the idea someone else needs. If the person who shares it with you gets negative feedback from you, that other person might not get to hear that idea that could help them!

So just say thank you. Then move on to the next person. Ask them the same question, get some ideas, say thank you, and continue.

Listen when someone shares. Write down their idea. Even if you wrote almost that exact same thing down before (because someone else said it), write it down again. When you see the same idea on your paper five times, that's a hint that maybe a lot of people see this idea. Chances are you did, too. If not, then it's even more valuable!

EVERYONE MAKES THEIR OWN CHOICE

This is often a challenge for leaders who are accustomed to exercising more direct control: Everyone makes their own choice.

You make your choice not just because you're a leader. You make your choice because you're a person. You're a Whole Person and you're living a Whole Life. You have to decide what you think will work for you. You have to decide what you think you can do. So does everyone else.

188

Of the ideas, what will you do? Maybe one. Maybe none. Maybe some combination of a few of them. You get to decide. The ideas are just ideas. They might help you come up with something new. They might give you an obvious path if a lot of people said the same thing.

Everyone gets to decide.

WHAT GETS MEASURED GETS DONE

When people know they will be asked about something later on, they remember things differently. When they know things will be measured later on, they do things differently. It's just how humans work.

Depending upon how often you have meetings, follow up on how people are doing. You can use the same Quantification to ask how they are doing at applying one or more ideas, or you can just ask a yes/no question. Check in with where you feel you are as a team at Month 1, Month 2, Month 3 and then at Month 6.

If the group decides some element of Ohana has hit the target of 8 or 9, you can put it on a "Done and Doing." That list just means you did it, and now it's a practice. Keep it on a list somewhere everyone will see so it reinforces that it's not "done and dropped," it's "Done and Doing." Then start with another aspect.

You can ask people to self-evaluate how they are doing on their individual thing. If they hit their target, they can keep their own "Done and Doing" list. Then they move on to their next thing.

Check in on overall Ohana as you go, too. You might have gotten Oasis up to a 9, but overall, Ohana is at a 7. Then the group may decide that now that people actually feel better when they get to work, they want to work on that Aloha thing, or maybe Harmony, or... whatever they choose!

If you have frequent enough meetings, weekly or more often, you might get to all aspects of Ohana in a year to a year and a half. If your meetings are monthly, it might take a few years. It won't four-fold the time because people will be improving in between meetings when it become a consistent thing.

New people will naturally integrate into the culture as it exists. The "Done and Doing" list and *The Ohana Way Report* or *The Ohana Way Book* will provide a framework for them.

Once you establish the pattern, your new group culture is just naturally going to be Ohana!

ABOUT THE AUTHOR

Scot Conway, Ph.D., J.D., Master Martial Artist

"Just one thing." That's all Conway claims to know. Yet he is prolific across so many topics! What does he mean by "just one thing"?

Conway has worked as an attorney at law, and a real estate broker, both licenses he continues to hold in the State of California, United States of America. He pastors at QX Church, teaches at the Guardian Quest Academy, counsels, mentors and coaches. He does keynote speaking, and organizational training. He writes books, and he also produces audio training programs. How is all that from "just one thing"?

It started with six-year-old Scot Conway walking into his first martial arts class holding his mother's hand. That quiet, shy, little first grade boy had no idea what lay before him. All he knew as a kid was that he wanted to be a super hero.

High school began to show a little of what he was made of. Earning his varsity letter, leading the gaming club, leading the school literary magazine, an officer in the fencing club, and winning the Patriot of the Year award hinted at things to come.

College would follow, with law school after that, and finally, a Ph.D. He'd have more involvement with organizations, presentations at conferences, teaching seminars across the USA and internationally, and being recruited to help start various projects. That first martial arts class would lead to master ranks, eventually to the highest rank allowed in his art to a person his age.

These days, there is a thing called Attention Deficit Disorder, and Conway fits the criteria - but he wields it as an asset. He did the same with his dyslexia. He was trained through his martial arts to harness his scattering mind to learn a great many things. He harnessed the way his brain flips things around to see the world differently. The end result is a man who has what appears to be a stunning breadth of knowledge and skill.

He calls it "just one thing" because it's all connected. No subject on which he writes, teaches, or trains exists in a vacuum.

There are common principles found in all of them that weave together and bind it all together. He breaks it up for us and teaches us how to apply these principles in area after area of our business, our relationships, our internal lives and the rest of life.

Read enough, listen enough, and train with Conway enough and you begin to see what he means. More importantly, you begin to see how to do it for yourself. That, ultimately, is Conway's goal. He does not desire to be our guru. He wants to facilitate us being our own guru, our own leader, and the master of our own lives.

Conway shares what he knows so we can make our own decisions and our own discoveries. His desire is to see us unleashed as true Masters of Life.

AVAILABILITY

Keynote Speaker
Corporate Trainer
Executive Advisor
Life Coach Trainer

WEBSITES/CONTACT

Not for Profit
QuestXian.org

Corporate Training
4P360.com

Programs
ScotWith1T.com
ScotConway.com
ScotConway.org

Martial Arts
GQDojo.com

Contact: Scot@ScotWith1T.com
Or through any of the above websites

Mailing Address
Scot Conway
2782-E Sweetwater Springs Blvd.
Spring Valley, CA 91977
(address current as of 2017)

BOOKS BY THE AUTHOR

Read other books by Scot Conway.

http://amzn.com/e/B009VNPT44

Or search: "Scot Conway" on Amazon.com

The Princess is a Knight

The Ohana Way Book: Shaping a Culture of Community. (https://amzn.com/B01GAL2RKI)

The Ohana Way Report: An Introduction to Shaping a Culture of Community. (https://amzn.com/B01G6K85Y0)

Emotional Genius: Exceptional Emotional Intelligence In Reach for Everyone with the Language of Emotions. (http://amzn.com/B00832FUZC)

Freedom Found: Five Step System to Let Go, Completely Forgive and Create Total Personal Freedom. (http://amzn.com/B0086QVUYA)

Above It All: A Toolbox to Let Go as You Go. (http://amzn.com/B00850W834)

The versions of the books for people of faith are *Complete Forgiveness* (http://amzn.com/B007XIFSOK) and *Not Of This World* (http://amzn.com/B007ZLD34M) written for the Christian audience.

MORE BOOKS BY THE AUTHOR

Hiring an Expert Speaker, Trainer or Coach: Get Extreme Value from Your Chosen Expert and Stay Within Your Budget. (http://amzn.com/B0089ZX2WQ)

Have It All 1: Law of Harmony: The Secret Gateway to Everything You Ever Wanted. (http://amzn.com/B007WOQN9E)

Have It All 2: Using the Law of Harmony for Wealth, Relationship, Body, Self, and Life. (http://amzn.com/B007WUWXYM)

Have It All 3: Law of Harmony: Living in Exponential Abundance Now. (http://amzn.com/B00E9G5UI8)

The Art, The Word, The Principles, The Character: The Lectures and Lessons of Guardian Karate. (http://amzn.com/B009978ATI)

The Body, The Skills, The Feelings, The Growth: The Lectures and Lessons of Guardian Jujutsu. (http://amzn.com/B00997JU6K)

The Self, The Weapons, The Spirit, The Becoming: The Lectures and Lessons of Guardian Kobujutsu. (http://amzn.com/B00997JS80)

Go to www.ScotWith1T.com to see if Conway has private reports or books available.

AUDIO PROGRAMS BY SCOT CONWAY

(List as of 2017)
http://www.ScotConway.com
http://www.ScotConway.org

OHANA 101 The Fundamentals of Family

Leadership 101 - 4P360 Leadership

YORI 101 - Relationship Trust Matrix
YORI 110 - YORI for Business
YORI 202 - Next Level Relationships
YORI 220 - Twenty-One Ways to Win

Emotional Genius: Language of Emotions 101a
Emotional Genius: Language of Emotions 101b

Pure Power 101 - Forgiveness and Beyond
Pure Power 202 - Beyond Forgiveness

Holographic Immersion Definitions

Power Matrix: Ultimate Values Workshop

Quest X Life Transformation System

Truly Unconditional Love

Complete and Unleashed: Next Level Masculinity and Femininity in the Modern World

Heroic Masculinity

Masculinity: Masculine Sexuality

Dating By The Book

PreCourting

God Says: Divorce is Okay (and everyone agrees)

Attention Deficit Solution

"The Talk"

Awesome Sex

Your review makes a difference!
Let us know something you learned!

Made in the USA
Lexington, KY
28 July 2019